Dear Mike,
this is almost a story. NEVER become a Mule!

THE CORPORATE MULE

Dont't Give Up Your Soul for the Company Goal

Live & Enjoy each Day
Be & Playl

Peace, your friend

A Novel by
Robert V. Gerard

Inner Eye Books
an imprint of
OUGHTEN HOUSE PUBLICATIONS
PO Box 2008
Livermore, CA 94551 USA

The Corporate Mule: Don't Give Up Your Soul
for the Company Goal
by Robert V. Gerard

Copyright © 1997 Robert Vincent Gerard

Published 1997.

03 02 01 00 99 98 97   10 9 8 7 6 5 4 3 2 1

This is a work of fiction. Any resemblance to persons living or dead is purely coincidental.

Published by

Inner Eye Books

an imprint of
OUGHTEN HOUSE PUBLICATIONS
PO Box 2008
LIVERMORE, CA 94551-2008
Phone: (510) 447-2332 Fax: (510) 447-2376
E-mail: oughtenhouse.com
Internet: www.oughtenhouse.com

Library of Congress Cataloging-in-Publication Data

Gerard, Robert V. (Robert Vincent), 1945-
The corporate mule : don't give up your soul for the company goal! /
    by Robert V. Gerard
            p.   cm.
    ISBN 1-880666-04-9 (alk. paper) $13.95
    1. Industrial relations—Fiction. 2. Office politics—Fiction. I. Title.
    PS3557.E637C6   1996
    813' .54—dc21   96-46572
                                            CIP

ISBN 1-880666-04-9, Trade Publication
Printed in United States of America
Printed with vegetable ink on acid-free paper

DEDICATION

This book is dedicated to all those (whether in heaven or hell) who gave up their soul for the company goal, to those employees who still have a chance and are able to read this story, and to those who are aware of the agony and life-killing stresses incurred daily because of their job.

This book is also dedicated to companies that advocate creative product development, individual self-development, and increased long-term relationships with their employees, and to the well-managed companies that perpetuate freedom, contribute to a nation's culture, adapt to planetary changes, and champion humane global economics.

This story is also about the pursuit of individual and organizational growth — together. Let us recognize and celebrate the unique contribution each makes and nurture the divine spark in everyone.

ACKNOWLEDGMENTS

When my nineteen year old son, Ryan, first read this manuscript, I found him giggling and cracking up as he turned the pages. I knew, then, that the truths hidden in this story had meaning for him. This book, then, is for Ryan, and all those who want to become an integrated part of our great society. Our children should be encouraged to explore their talents and pursue their dreams. Their minds yearn to be recognized. By our own example, we must show our children that learning is the *process* of life. When the teenager realizes that personal growth *is* success, then success is no longer a *goal*; it becomes only one aspect of life.

Transcribing creative thoughts and imagery was only made possible by the dedication, loyalty, and support provided by my dear friends and by their editorial assistance with the manuscript.

It gives me great pleasure to honor them, their keen insights and timely responses. My heartfelt gratitude goes out to Gené Virginia Long, Valerie Kegebein, Charlie Behan, Judy Kay Scott, and to the late Sonia Cordill of the Writers Bloc; to my dear friend, Jacqueline LaValle, for her candid comments; and to my darling wife, Anita, who was always at my side.

Special mention needs to be given to Les Mound, Tony Stubbs, and Marilyn Pesola who offered critical feedback as to the feelings, intent, and accuracy of the manuscript.

One Hundred Years Ago

Crazy old Jonny MacGregor, a senile ex-Cavalry Civil War soldier, sat atop his beloved mule, Scotty, and squinted his eyes, wishing he could see around the bend in the road. "Damn," he mumbled. "My eyes ain't what they used ta be. Cottonwood ought to be around here somewhere."

Scotty bobbed his head in agreement as MacGregor sent a wad of brown juice flying out the side of his mouth. What didn't clear his mouth settled on top of the caked remnants of previous spits, streaking his gray beard a motley brown.

"Too bad the war's over, Scotty," MacGregor said sadly. "We still got a lot of fight left in us. Shame ta waste it."

Scotty let out a snort as they plodded on.

"You know, Scotty, a man's gotta have a war to fight. Keeps him fit. That's why we're headed west, to fight them Indians. Keep an eye out, Scotty. Might be Indians hiding up there. Mighty purtty country 'round here, ain't it, boy?" MacGregor turned his dusty felt hat so that the tacked up brim rested over his left ear. The hat now shaded his wrinkled eyes from the relentless sun.

They cleared the bend and MacGregor saw smoke curling from chimneys a quarter of a mile away. "Must be Cottonwood, Scotty. The end of our long ride from Atlanta."

As they turned onto Jericho Street, MacGregor heard gunshots. He unsheathed his rifle from the saddle scabbard and kicked Scotty's ribs. "Wowee, Scotty! A fight. Let's go!"

Scotty side-stepped from the sudden kicks to his ribs. He laid his ears back, danced in circles, and brayed hysterically.

"Damn it, Scotty, this ain't no time ta balk! I said let's go! There's a fight brewin'. Let's move!"

As MacGregor got closer, he saw two masked men running from the bank. Each carried a canvas sack in one hand and a revolver in the other. They shot randomly as citizens scurried for cover. One robber's horse, a black stallion, caught a bullet to the head from the deputy sheriff's rifle just as the robber mounted. The horse fell to the ground as though the street were pulled out from under it.

"Shit!" the robber yelled, "my *gawd*-damned horse!"

In the midst of the crossfire, Scotty danced in circles between the bandits and the sheriff as MacGregor struggled to shoulder his rifle and rein Scotty in the right direction.

The second robber's horse spun around and the masked bandit saw MacGregor raise the rifle to his shoulder and take aim. He fired his revolver at MacGregor just as Scotty circled again. The bullet caught MacGregor in the back.

"Damn the horse!" the second thief hollered. "Grab that stupid old mule!"

The first robber jumped onto Scotty, dug his shiny spurs into the mule's ribs, and the robbers haphazardly clattered down the newly cobbled street. Scotty bucked and brayed, showing long, yellow teeth, while trying to dislodge the stranger on his back.

The last thing MacGregor remembered was aiming his gun. He awoke to find himself before a beautiful glowing lady. The light emanating from her was so bright he could barely make out her features.

"Come," she said inside his head.

He found himself flying at great speed through a tunnel. At the end of the long tunnel the figure said, "Look."

MacGregor saw himself lying on the cobbled street, watching his beloved mule kicking up his heels and braying something awful. MacGregor's heart wrenched. Scotty was the only living thing he had ever loved. They had been together more than twenty years.

"Look here," the lady said.

MacGregor turned his head and saw a baby emerging from his mother. He didn't know how he knew it was his mother, but he knew. In an instant he saw everything he had ever done, felt every vile word he had ever spoken in the life just ended. There were a few good words, mostly for Scotty, although he'd done his share of cussing at that stubborn old mule. He cringed. It was not a pretty sight.

They went through another tunnel, the beautiful lady lighting the way with her bright inner light. Then MacGregor was shown pictures of another life, one that took place in the Middle Ages when he was a knight and where his only attachment was to a horse. He saw his inability to feel love or commit to people, saw the safety in loving only an animal. Then the pictures of both lives were shown side by side and MacGregor thought, "How awful. I have not accomplished anything in either of those lives."

"You have the power to change that," the lady said, knowing his thoughts. Then she showed him a picture one hundred years into the future where a perfect opportunity to overcome his anti-social behavior would present itself to him. The people and circumstances in that future period would enable him to accept love as well as give it. It would help him grow so that he could then help others.

The lady brought him to the edge of a third tunnel, one so brightly lit that MacGregor could hardly believe what he saw. Before him a golden city beckoned. Waves of love washed over him, enveloping him in ways he couldn't describe. He was drawn closer and closer to the golden gate. As they drew nearer the gate, he knew he'd never want to leave this place. He begged to be allowed to stay, if even for a just little while.

"Not at this time," the lady said. "This is what awaits those who love." Her arm swept along the sparkling landscape just beyond reach, so close yet so far away.

MacGregor saw that his next life would not be an easy one. His spirit guide gave him two options for his next life: He could grow by setting up a simple life and learning to love in its uncomplicated framework. Or he could choose a more difficult path of setting high standards for himself and hopefully coming to realize how hollow they were. Perhaps then he would realize that loving himself and others was what the game was all about.

He chose the latter. He would come into a family steeped in mediocrity on Long Island, New York. The desire to learn, serve, love, and be fulfilled would not be given much expression. But his father would lay high expectations on him which McGregor could not possibly meet. The big question was: Could he break through and discover that only love really mattered?

He had one hundred years to map out every step of that life. MacGregor would put many obstacles in his path for the reward was like none he had ever imagined.

CHAPTER 1

REBIRTH

It was the last day of my last semester as an undergraduate student that life began to hold some promise for me. I majored in Business Administration at a conservative business college near Atlanta and had done quite well. I was surprised because my first year at college was rudderless. The freedom of being away from a complaining mother and a dominant father for the first time was a heady experience. Parties and beautiful Southern girls occupied most of my time. Born and bred in New York, the South was a cultural shock but in time, after the newness wore off and familiarity set in, I settled down and applied myself. I had made the Dean's List consistently this past year. Look out business world, here I come! I am going to be someone, no matter what my father says.

It hurt that my parents never once in four years ventured off Long Island to visit me. I suppose, being New Yorkers, they viewed Georgians as a land of hostile rednecks. They wouldn't want to chance upon an unexpected lynching on one of Atlanta's tranquil streets. Though they paid for my education, they didn't seem to care much about it one way or the other. My father always said I'd never amount to much.

But now I was on the first rung of that corporate ladder that had been my dream since high school. I had an interview at CSC, a large computer company, after my next class. As I hurried down the hall to the classroom, I thought about the call I had made to my father about the up-coming interview.

"Don't get your hopes up, boy," he had begun. "Just because you have an interview doesn't mean you have the job. But if you get it, keep your nose to the grindstone, do what they tell you, and soon you'll be telling others what to do. That's what success is."

It was more or less the response I had expected, yet it left that odd feeling in the pit of my stomach where my father was concerned, an endless hole I'd always tried to fill but didn't know how. He had always pounded into me that he was a failure and that I would do no better than him. I'm sure he felt that the station he occupied in life was beneath him. He had never been able to become more than a senior loan officer at Hempstead Bank in Long Island and he resented it. He blamed his failure on everyone else, including my mother and myself. Well, I'd show him. I planned to succeed all by myself. That way if I failed, I'd have no one to blame. A real man would shoulder that kind of responsibility himself. Why blame the wife and kids? I always felt that he hated being told what to do and that's why he was such a tyrant at home. It was the only place where he could lord it over others.

"Hi, Scott."

I'd been so lost in my thoughts that I didn't see Diane until she stopped in front of me and I almost walked into her. She was a lovely Southern brunette but she was looking to get married. With some women, that's all they wanted in life—a husband and kids.

"I haven't seen you in a while. Where have you been hiding?"

I looked at my watch. "I don't have time to talk now, Di. I'll be late for class. I'll call you. Soon," I said, making a fast getaway.

Diane had been my first "score" in college. Because of her I had looked at all Southern women as a way to score but I soon found out that what they really wanted was to saddle you down with a house and kids. Not for me, thank you. When I told Di that I had no intention of settling down, she seemed hurt. I think she really cared for me but I had other plans. For the time being, they didn't include a woman by my side.

I made it to class just as Mr. Simmons, the assistant professor of my Management class, announced that today's guest speaker, who was already a few minutes late, would lecture on "The Changing Values in the Work Place."

"Professor," I said, "work values shouldn't change. Isn't it expected that every employee will perform his best all the time and advance as much as possible?"

"It used to be that way, Scott. But today's workers have a different attitude. Anyway, Mr. Goldberg of AT&T, a world leader in the telecommunications industry, will give you a firsthand look at what's happening in the work force today."

Moments later, Mr. Goldberg arrived. The class acknowledged his authority and accepted his words without reservation. The mood was apparent: a heavenly disciple had descended to prepare us for the business messiah. My classmates and I honed in on the lecture. Mostly clean-shaven faces and well-trimmed hairlines exemplified ambition to earn membership into the multi-layered business of power and profit.

The class listened attentively, except for Jerry and Marlene. Jerry appeared annoyed. Much older than his classmates, Jerry was out of sync with the group. A bearded, long-haired ex-hippie, he was a junior majoring in Human Resources Management. Two seats behind him sat a despondent Marlene, a black female whose major was Music. God only knows why she was in this class.

Goldberg's lecture focused on generating and maintaining a high-quality employee base. He offered specifics on competence, performance, and allegiance to the company. At the conclusion of the lecture, he invited questions. As usual, the class remained silent, appearing occupied with intent contemplation. Simmons prodded them on. Finally, one senior ventured, "Mr. Goldberg, you said that many college graduates are very ambitious and eager to make a good impression on their first job."

"Yes, I did."

"Then how long does it take them to realize the truth and return to a normal level of work activity like everyone else?"

"That's a good question," Goldberg replied. "We try to look at that event as the time of the second grooming, when more responsibility is given to the individual."

"Are you saying, sir," Jerry asked, "that you actually take advantage of the new recruit until he or she rebels?"

"Excuse me," Goldberg replied, "but what do you mean by 'take advantage of'?"

"I mean, giving the recruit the lowest possible pay, the greatest amount of hype, and the most tedious work."

"Absolutely not! Where did you get that idea?"

The class grunted. Goldberg's validity and pride were at stake. A murmur arose.

Enough's enough, I thought so I spoke up in Goldberg's defense. "Class, I believe that what Mr. Goldberg is trying to say is that we are important to the world of business. It's young people like us that keep the spirit of free enterprise alive. Just think, some day one of us might become the vice president of a large corporation. Right?" Why I hadn't gone all the way to the top was beyond me.

Marlene's voice was soft but what she said was loud enough for everyone to hear. "Listen, child, you give your soul to the company and they'll sell it for a profit."

Chapter 2

THE CORPORATE FAMILY

The third Monday after graduation was a beautiful June day in Atlanta. Outside CSC's corporate headquarters, I walked among fourteen college recruits from the Human Resources Training Center to the corporate office across the street.

The giant glass doors swung open and we entered the magnificent world of big business. The corporate lobby glittered with marketing and first-impression paraphernalia. I was in ecstasy.

Each of us, as new employees, wore a large name tag as we were to be met by our respective managers. My future manager had no trouble identifying me; he grinned like a child running loose in a toy store.

"Hi, Scott. I'm Tom McClane, your manager. Welcome aboard." McClane was a pudgy little guy with a bushy mustache. His tie was a bit crooked and his jacket was unbuttoned.

"Good morning, Mr. McClane," I said, surprised that he was not what I would consider well-dressed. We shook hands and my career officially began.

As we walked down the long hallway, McClane gave me the entire rundown, everything I needed to know about employee orientation. No problem, I thought. I've studied extremely hard and proved that I was an independent achiever. It should be easy to achieve success here.

The computer center was huge and hummed with a high-pitched whine. McClane pointed out the huge mainframe computer and an impressive assortment of terminals. Various laser and tractor-feed printers spat out reams of paper. He introduced me to the three people responsible for operating the computers. "They're good people to know and to have on your side," he said once we left the electronic hive.

I was puzzled by that. Wasn't everyone on the same side? As we approached the elevators, I asked, "What's our floor?"

"The sixth."

Just then the elevator doors opened and several young, well-dressed people emerged to scurry past me. We got in the carpeted elevator. After a moment of silence, the doors quietly closed and we began our ascent to the sixth floor. Neither McClane nor I spoke.

The doors opened on the third floor and a young, sharply-dressed man entered reading an upscale marketing magazine. "Mr. McClane," he said, looking up and nodding his head in McClane's direction. "How are you doing?" His voice was clear and confident voice.

"Hello, Brian. I'm just fine," McClane answered genially.

Brian looked like a million, from his double-breasted dark suit and polished shoes to his perfectly blow-dried hair. He was a real Fifth Avenue model. For a moment I experienced a twinge of homesickness.

"Tom," Brian said, breaking the hushed silence, "when you've got a minute, I'd like to share something with you."

"Sure, Brian. How about ten o'clock?"

"Good. I'll see you in my office."

The elevator stopped on the fifth floor and Brian walked out, all of his attention devoted to his magazine.

When the elevator doors closed once again, McClane turned to me and said, "Brian's the Director of Marketing."

I imagined myself in that position but before I ask any questions, the elevator stopped on our floor. The silver and black doors opened to reveal a dark-haired woman sitting behind a large, circular desk. As we walked toward her, she focused her eyes on my crotch, her jaw very busy with chewing gum. I didn't know if it was best to acknowledge her interest or play it cool. I looked elsewhere, but McClane nudged me, bringing me closer to the woman.

"Hi, Maria," McClane joyfully said to the big-eyed girl. "I'd like to introduce you to a new member to our staff. This is Scott Hendrick, a recent college graduate. Scott, meet Maria, our receptionist and the only woman on this floor aggressive enough to be dangerous."

"Let him find out for himself," Maria said, dropping her eyes to my crotch again. "Hi, there, Scotty. It's nice to see a tall, good looking man like you around here," she said with a lascivious grin.

"Good to meet you, too, Maria." My mouth suddenly seemed to fill with foam and I was stuck for words. I was relieved when McClane said, "Well, you'll be seeing enough of each other soon. See you later, Maria."

We walked down the corridor and McClane stopped outside a doorway. He proudly pointed his hand in, stepped aside, and said, "Here's your office, Mr. Hendrick."

I looked inside the nine by nine, gray on gray cubicle. The walls were bare except for the tape marks and nail holes accumulated from previous occupants. In the center of the room, facing the door, was a beat up blonde wooden desk with a phone and a worn leather executive's chair. The drab gray carpeting was well worn and coffee stained in the area around the chair.

My mouth sagged open. I had expected something bigger, with better furnishings.

"What you need to do next, young man," McClane said, "is to get some supplies. Call Carol, the department's office assistant, and she'll give you more insight on what you'll need."

I put my new black attaché case on the desk. My mouth was still dry. I needed a drink of something badly.

"Oh!" McClane said before leaving, "if anyone asks, your job responsibility code is two-nine-oh-oh-one. Also, when you get settled in, come and see me."

"Yes, sir," I said, sitting down behind my desk.

I sat at my desk in a sort of hollow fascination. I was the proud owner of a used room. The desk had a large chip on the right hand corner and various scratches everywhere. Someone must have swapped the chair because, besides being broken, it definitely did not match. When I leaned back in it, I almost fell over backward. Then I noticed the ultimate disrespect: a cigarette burn right in the middle of the desk.

The phone rang. "Hi, Mr. Hendrick," a pleasant voice said. "This is Carol. If at all possible, can you please come and see me? My desk is at the southeast corner of the building."

"Sure. I'll be right there." She definitely sounded sweet and I wanted to check her out. As I prepared to leave, I made sure my briefcase covered the burnt crater. The southeast corner? Where the hell was that? I needed a compass.

When I arrived, after asking directions, Carol was not there. Her desk was located outside the large corner office of Ira Eastman, a senior vice president. His office was swanky and official. It represented prestige and power.

Then the sweetest sound I'd heard all day echoed from behind me. "Hi, Mr. Hendrick."

I turned around and lost it instantly. Knees buckling, balls rumbling, cottonmouth tripping me up, I responded clumsily with, "Er ... uh, I'm Scott."

Carol was beautiful. Her Southern face and soft hazel eyes mesmerized me. Her body was slender and delicate. I mean perfect. She smiled, seeming to understand my dilemma. When she stared into my eyes, my knees got weaker as all the blood rushed into my head. My palms were sweaty. With the barest drop of moisture on my tongue I managed to say, "Sure glad I got this job. You make it all worthwhile." I even managed a weak smile.

I settled down when I saw that Carol was all business. She was a great help and offered her insight on what I needed to set up my office. Then she gave me a brief tour of the facilities. In the kitchen, I was shown the "public" cups and the "do not touch" personal mugs. She pointed to the kitchen rules posted over the sink with the large headline: FOLLOW OR BE KILLED!

"Go ahead," she said, "read it."

When I read the paragraph that said, "Coffee stains, sugar spills, messy counter tops, overflowing garbage cans, uncleaned tables, and rotten food in the refrigerator will not be tolerated." I was surprised that she had written it.

After forty minutes of Carol's orientation, and me fantasizing about awesome sex with my tour guide, I poured a cup of coffee and headed back to my office. As I entered, the phone was ringing. "It's me," a female voice announced abruptly. It certainly wasn't Carol's soft, sweet voice.

"Me, who?"

"Boy, Scotty, you forget fast." There was a hint of antagonism in her voice.

"Is this Maria?"

"It's about time. Listen, kid. You'll need to call the telephone department and get your personal extension number set up. I need to know your number immediately so that I can log it in my book in case someone is trying to call and I—"

"Okay! Okay! I'll do it right now," I said. Maria had irritated me from the beginning and now she'd pushed all thoughts of eloping with Carol out of my mind.

I stared at the phone after hanging up and thought that her phone manners were appalling. I recalled my last interview with the personnel recruiter. He had emphasized that CSC was a highly visible computer software company and that, technically, CSC made the best products. It had recently begun a major campaign as a market-driven corporation and had a good reputation for employee development.

Following Carol's instructions, I made my way to the supply room on the tenth floor. My next encounter with another true Southern belle occurred thirty seconds after I pressed the assistance button. Time stopped. Ultra-low vibrations overwhelmed me, as if *Battlestar Galactica* hovered above me. Succulent lips, bright blue eyes, and a well-filled, red sweater. A goddess was before me and I stood there like an ass.

"Yes?" she said.

"Yes," I said.

"Yes what?" she asked.

I couldn't speak. Visions of ecstatic unions with the lovely form before me rendered me speechless.

"Can I help you?" she asked again, slightly annoyed.

Still captivated, I managed to stutter, "I...I, er, I'd like this requisition filled."

Encounters with females were everywhere. I hoped I would get used to it. Unpredictably, my mind was caught in a totally new juxtaposition: career versus women. The office environment was quite different to the relatively cloistered one of high school or college. The women were more poised and sure of themselves and their sexuality. It certainly wasn't like any of the TV programs I thought had mirrored life when I was a kid.

I thought for a moment on my early education through television, the only constant source of visual non-dysfunctional learning in my dysfunctional family. Television had been just about my only friend.

Alex P. Keaton of *Family Ties* had been my idol, my role model. He was so suave, sophisticated, and smart. Although Alex focused on politics, I always knew I would focus on business. I would grow up to be a taller version of Alex P. Keaton, just as smart, just as sophisticated, and just as successful with the ladies.

I had a surge of machismo then, when a realization hit me: Atlanta's ratio of women to men was about five to one.

Chapter 3

WASH THOSE BRAINS

The weekend rainstorm continued as it brought havoc to the early Monday morning rush hour traffic, but I didn't care. The traffic jams had no effect on me, either. I felt really good. I'd blown over three hundred dollars out of my first paycheck over the weekend and still had money left over. My eleven-year-old green Ford was fully paid for, I had a great job, a lot of new clothes, no serious commitments, no kids. I'd be rich in a couple of years and that was what I wanted. I felt very smug about my future.

In the cramped elevator that smelled of musty raincoats and wet newspaper umbrellas, I was forced to listen to complaints about children, spouses, the lack of time to do anything worthwhile, and Monday mornings. Most of all, my co-workers complained about never having enough money. Oblivious to their gloom, satisfaction with my career put me above it all. My grin became annoying to them.

"Hey, Scott," taunted Fred Joyner, the sixth-floor wise-guy. "What kind of drug are you on this morning?"

I didn't appreciate the muffled chuckles. I looked down at Fred, a half-pint whose inverted upper lip curled with pessimism. "Why, Mr. Joyner, I am delighted to be here."

Hoots and hisses followed my declaration.

"Sixth floor! We're out of here!" Fred shouted as the doors opened.

The elevator emptied out people who should have bright-eyed and ready to meet the work day. Instead, they moved slowly, human robots marching off to their offices, too heavy from a weekend off to function or pay attention to their goals, if they had any.

Back in my office, I noticed that the rain had left spots on my new shoes. I grabbed a tissue and began wiping them clean when there was a loud knock on my door, startling me. The door crashed open to admit a ferocious looking, red-haired guy; a body-builder and real jock, I thought.

"Hi!" he said affably. "My name is Doug. I just came by to officially welcome the new recruit."

"Well, that's nice of you, Doug."

"Actually, Scott, I came by to see if you were another wimp just out of college."

I pursed my lips and eyed him steadily.

"What's the matter, boy? Did I hurt your feelings?"

I had to make a stand or else be known as a wimp. "No, not really." I replied. "You just threw me off a little."

"A lot, it looked to me."

"Well, so what? What do you want?"

"Listen, boy. Don't mind me. I act tough on the outside, feel tough on the inside, and play tough all the time."

"Yeah, right." I scoffed. What kind of trip was this guy into anyway? He kept staring at me. I had to say something. "I'm glad you're tough, Doug."

"You're okay, Scott."

Tom McClane walked up to the door just as the scrimmage between Doug and me was cooling down. The most powerful of us all, Tom was the shortest, the pudgiest, and the most out-of-shape. He looked up at Doug and needled him. "Hey, shithead, did you get the compiler installed yet?"

"Fuck, no. I'll need one more day."

"Damn!" Tom said with annoyance. "Try to get it done soon or we'll both have other problems to deal with."

Doug left and Tom strolled into my office, stretched out in the chair, and propped his feet on my desk.

Their crude language, their unorthodox business mannerisms—and Tom's feet on my desk—conflicted with my concept of the workplace: slick, smooth operations and big deals going down all the time.

"Don't forget the ten o'clock New Employee Orientation meeting today," Tom reminded me.

I responded instantly, without too much thought. "Oh, no, sir. I can't wait to see the Chief Executive Officer and the other senior executives."

"Well, don't get too high on all the crap they hand you."

"Why?" I asked in disbelief.

"Just listen and listen carefully. Read between the lines and try to see the big picture. Remember, always keep your identity and get a feel for where you fit in."

"I don't understand what you are getting at, Mr. McClane."

"Call me Tom."

"Yes, sir."

"Now, Scott, this is your first job, is it not?"

"Yes, sir."

"You will be learning a lot of new things. Take your time and learn one thing at a time. Always keep in mind one thing: it's not *what* you know, it's *who* you know. Just remember, if you get a bad label stamped on your forehead, it's yours, so you might as well pack it in."

The New Employee Orientation meeting was a real snazzy show put on for the new recruits' benefit. The presenters were John Mayes, the CEO; Ed Vernan, the executive vice president; Ira Eastman, my division's senior vice president; Ken Michael, the Director of Human Resources; and Grant Fretman, the Director of Training and Development.

As I settled myself into a front row chair in the conference room, there was a moment of silence before the show began. I was alert and attentive, looking steadily at the gods of CSC, hoping that one, maybe two, would recognize my offer of servitude and loyalty, and reciprocate.

Human Resources opened the program with a quick introduction. I was fired up and ready for the CEO. I took the opportunity to introduce myself to the girl who was sitting next to me. "Hi. I'm Scott."

She offered a quick smile and said, "Hi. My name is Kama."

We didn't get beyond introductions because the program started, but I felt comfortable sitting next to her.

"Welcome, all," the mighty Mr. Mayes said as he approached the podium. "You're here to join us in a profitable enterprise. We are more than pleased to have you with us."

The CEO's speech lasted a mere twenty-two minutes, during which he offered an idealistic vision. "The bottom line is clear, my friends: It's you. Yes, *people* are the key to a successful business and higher profits."

Then Mayes, who was well aware of the zest and eagerness of his audience, crystallized the motivating process by planting a challenge. "It's really up to you, each and every one of you. Ask yourself these questions. Do you want to have a successful career? Do you want to have that lovely house? Do you want to have that new high-priced car? Do you enjoy expensive vacations? Then, my friends, here is the opportunity to prove yourselves. Do you understand your mission at CSC? Thank you all."

After the applause, Ken Michaels said, "Okay, folks, it's time for a little break. We have plenty of coffee and donuts in the adjoining room. Let's take ten minutes."

We needed a carbo rush and CSC knew it. There were plenty of donuts, coffee, and chocolate cookies for everyone. I was excited and ready to hear more from the execs.

Just as I gulped down my second donut, Fretman began to herd the group back into the fancy conference room. He got everyone to sit down again and trumpeted yet another famous quotation from his gallery of resources. "When a fellow says, 'It ain't the money but the principle of the thing,' you can bet it's the money."

While the audience chuckled, Ira Eastman walked up to the platform without any introduction. He adjusted his wire-rimmed glasses and scanned the group until the audience grew silent. His stocky body was wrapped in an expensive blue pin-striped suit and his round pink face betrayed nothing as he looked at us. His voice was flat as he said, "What a cooperative group of fine young professionals."

I hoped it was an expression of appreciation for our potential but I heard a quiet snort from Kama, the recruit sitting next to me. I examined her profile out of the corner of my eye. Gently I nudged her arm and whispered, "Gee, Kama, I'm amazed at how well these executives are tuned in to our needs."

She leaned her head toward me and grunted, "I don't think so."

She was a small-framed woman, athletically built. She had pretty features and smooth skin. The sprinkling of freckles across her face were endearing. Her carrot-colored hair flowed easily over most of her back.

My mouth fell open as she turned away from me. She didn't seem to be enthused with what she had heard so far.

During our carbo break, we started up a conversation. She told me that she was a native Californian. A graduate of Stanford University, she had received honors in her major, Entrepreneurial Management. Her opinion about CSC's executives was definitely different than mine.

At the end of the meeting, each recruit had an opportunity to shake hands with the senior managers. At that time, each recruit received a lapel pin—a dollar sign superimposed over a key. Purchased exclusively from Tiffany's, the pin exemplified the company's motto: Key people create profit.

Ten minutes later, I was sitting in my office when the phone rang. "Scott," Kama said, "you seemed annoyed with me during the meeting. I just wanted to clear up things between us."

"No, Kama. It was just your girlish behavior." I knew I was slightly off target when I heard her grunt.

Kama took a deep breath and said, "Look, I just wanted to share a few thoughts with you. That's all."

Maybe she wanted to get to know me better. "Sure, Kama. I'd like to spend some time with you and get to know you better, too."

"Scott, what I'm trying to say is, I think you're a nice looking guy."

"Hey, thanks, Kama. I think you're a pretty lady yourself."

"Yeah, I gathered that from the way you kept looking at me in the meeting."

"It seemed like you were trying to ignore me or fight me off or something."

"No, not really. Just being cautious, so to speak. I don't have many friends in Atlanta. As a matter of fact, I'm quite alone and you remind me of a little kid who's optimistic and ready to play. I could use a little of that zest in my life."

"Right you are."

A long moment of silence followed my reply.

"Scott, do you understand what I'm saying?"

"Sure."

"No, really. Do you?" she asked again. "I thought you might be interested in sharing a little about yourself, too."

"Oh, I am. I'm delighted you called. Maybe tomorrow, over lunch, you and I can talk about the orientation meeting."

"Yuck! Not that stuff!" she protested.

Kama wanted to get to know me. I wanted to talk business. Without too much consideration for her intentions, I said, "Some day you'll realize how motivating that entire meeting really was."

I must have hit her hot button because she responded with, "Don't be so ignorant, Mr. College. That meeting was a farce. If you fall for all that hype, you're going to be in it—*real* deep!"

"Listen here, Kama," I shot back, "You seem to forget where you are and who signs your paycheck."

"I think you are forgetting who *you* are, Scott."

"You're a reactionary, Kama"

"What?" Shock was evident in her voice, and by the silence that followed.

"Wake up, Kama. If you want to succeed, you must follow the leaders all the way. They've made it and I'm going to make it. But it's people like you who are going to have problems all too soon." I was unmovable.

"Damn it, Scott, you're as stupid as an old mule!"

That bothered me a lot. "You should talk!"

During every encounter with Kama after that first day, I tried to figure her out but couldn't. She irritated me yet I was drawn to her. There was no denying that we were attracted to each other. I felt her energy each time we met and saw her face light up with an inner glow. But she hated to talk about CSC and became easily rattled every time I did. Every time we spoke about CSC, an argument inevitably followed. She was just too hot-headed, and too outspoken for me to handle.

Chapter 4

LOYALTY AND DEDICATION

A voice from the doorway jolted me from my work. "Hey, shithead," Doug joked, "how about me taking you out for some Mexican to celebrate your first year of survival?"

"Sounds good to me." I tossed back, putting my files away. I grabbed my jacket and went with him.

On the way to the restaurant, Doug opened the console compartment in his car and pulled out a joint. "Want a toke?"

"Not me."

"It's your anniversary, stupid."

"No thanks. It's not business-like."

"Fool. Half the smoke and coke in the world is consumed by us business jerks."

"Damn it, Doug, you're always on my case."

Doug shook his head at the rebuff. He mocked me sarcastically with, "Okay, Doug, back off, back off."

Despite the bad start, our lunch hour was pleasant enough. Graced by a cool June breeze, we grabbed an outside table at Los Rajas and watched Atlanta's finest beauties stroll by.

"How do you feel about CSC after one year?" Doug asked.

"Four thousand dollars richer."

Doug's eyes widened in surprise. "You've got four grand stashed already?"

"Yep! And no big bills, either."

"I wish I had the opportunity to start all over again," he said a little wistfully. "So, what's your plan?"

The waitress came for our order. Doug ordered his usual ale and the special of the day with extra fried beans, cheese, and hot sauce. I ordered a lite beer three tacos without beans and, mild sauce.

"Let's see," I continued as though the waitress hadn't appeared. "For starters, I think I'm going to get a new car. Possibly a BMW three-twenty-eight-i, or a Mustang GT, and maybe take a vacation up to the Williamsburg Restoration in Virginia."

"Invest the shit" Doug said, taking a long swallow of ale. "Buy a house or some good stocks, or real estate."

"Look, Doug, at the rate I'm saving money and with all the promotions to come, what do I have to worry about?"

"You're really dumb, kid. Do you know that? All I ever hear from your security-ridden mouth is what you have or what you're gonna have. You never talk about how you feel about things, unless it has to do with work. Don't you have a life outside of work? Will the real Scott Hendrick please stand up?"

"Get off my case, Doug. I've been through four years of college and ten tons of training. Now I have some good job experience. What can go wrong?"

"Stop being so naive." He belched loudly. "Wait 'til you have a wife and a family, plenty of bills and crap like that."

"You're a pessimist."

"Okay. Forget it."

Doug was frustrated with me. Even more so, I think he was frustrated with himself. He was getting close to his fortieth birthday and had two teenage daughters and a big house. The poor guy probably was in debt up to his ass.

"Ah," I said, rubbing my hands in anticipation, "here's our lunch." I waited while the food was put in front of us and then went on. "So far CSC has been treating me just great. I think I'm going to get a twenty-five percent increase in salary because Tom gave me an excellent evaluation."

"Twenty-five percent is an unheard of thing around here, Scott. Did Tom tell you that?"

"Indirectly." I took a bite of the first taco and chewed loudly. "He said my attendance is almost perfect, I dress well, I

do good work—more work than is expected of me—and I co-operate very well with my peers. All except you, that is."
"Thanks. Go on." He pushed the food around on his plate but ordered a second ale.
"Tom also said the quality of my work is exceptional and that usually brings in a better merit raise."
"What merit raise?"
"Performance," I said around a mouthful of the last taco. "The more you work, the more money you make."
"That's if you own your own business, Scott. The only ones who are going to make more money from all of your work are the executives and the stockholders." He drained the rest of the first ale and took a long swallow of the second.
"You just don't see the big picture, Doug."
"Skip it, Scott. How were your tacos?"
"Fine. How come you didn't eat everything?"
"Not that hungry, I guess."
Despite all the ruckus between Doug and me, the food was great, the women were stunning, and we were easily forty minutes late for work.

My first year had flown by. I was settled in and comfortable. Atlanta was an okay town. It was very clean and, compared to New York City, it was an easy place to live. Doug had been absolutely right. I had gotten CSC's normal five percent raise, but there was an added fringe benefit: plenty of women.
Being single was quite an advantage. It provided me with a multitude of opportunities to meet some really wonderful women. Everywhere I went, women gave me the eye. Slowly I began to realize that attempts to score undercut the possibilities for a longer-term, meaningful relationship. I was getting tired of one-nighters. Dating was too expensive and long, late-night outings were beginning to interfere with my ability to concentrate at work.

Daydreaming at my desk one morning, the ringing phone brought me back to reality. "Hi, Scott. Steve here. You got a few minutes to go over your training schedule with me?"

"Yeah, sure. How's now?"

"Good. Come to my office."

I eagerly picked up my leather-trimmed pocket calendar and an assortment of training memos and headed out of the office. Kama was leaving Ira Eastman's office and heading in the same direction. I waited for her. I looked at her sideways and said in my best Humphrey Bogart voice, "Where are you going, sweetheart?"

"Sweetheart, my foot. You're such an ass!"

"Ooooh, *touchy!*"

Kama stopped and turned toward me as if to retaliate. I looked down and saw the full curve of her breast swelling out of her low-cut silk blouse. When she caught my glance, she looked at me with disgust and stormed off into the lobby.

"Women!" I spat out in exasperation.

I proceeded to Steve's office down the hall. Despite my irritation with Kama, my optimistic attitude towards the job returned. I approached Steve's office with a grin. "Hey, Steve."

The slender Southerner's room was loaded with outdoorsman artifacts, most of which were related to some aspect of fishing. A large bass mounted on the wall was flanked by two similarly stuffed rainbow trout. Thank God he didn't have a moose over his desk.

Lazily leaning back into his chair, he fiddled with some kind of lure as he looked up at me. "And what are you so happy about, my Yankee friend?"

"Oh, things are just great around here," I happily said.

"You've got to be kidding," Steve muttered, more to himself than to me. He focused on the task at hand and said, "We need to discuss your training schedule for the next three months. Did you bring your training agenda?"

"Yep. Here it is." While Steve scanned the documents, I used those few moments to entertain myself with the decor. Then Kama came to mind. "Hey, Steve, how's Kama doing?"

"She's a fuckin' rebel broad."

"You're absolutely right."

Steve's blue eyes peered intently into mine. "You're just the opposite, Scott."

"What do you mean by that?"

"She's advanced herself more than any of the recruits who came in with y'all. She's way ahead of the rest of you in regard to workload, training, and performance. Ira Eastman has noticed her and speaks highly about her, but her attitude stinks. She's hot one day and cold the next. Sometimes she cares, sometimes she doesn't. When she speaks to me, I get the feeling that she doesn't give a damn about this place. Know what I mean, Scotty?"

"Sure do, Steve. That's women for you. They really belong back in the home with the kids and stuff. If you let them get the upper hand, you've got a ton of trouble." To me, business—especially management—was still strictly a guy thing.

"Yeah, they're not too good at camping, either," Steve grunted, obviously harboring some secret on that topic.

He fiddled with the lure some more and then said, "On the other hand, you're different, Scotty. You're very pro on the job. Your work attitude is always—and I mean *always*—super positive. You see it as a means of gaining success and accomplishing your goals."

"You'd better believe it," I said.

"You always want to do things right. You take the least chances and risks, study relentlessly, and hope to be recognized. Simply speaking, Scotty, you don't make any waves or get in the way of any politics."

"I'm happy to hear that, Steve. I'd like to know when I can get out of all this training activity and get down to some real good work."

"What's wrong with the training?"

"It's been on and off all year. All I ever seem to do is go to this training class or that training class. Sometimes I feel that I'm getting the simple stuff to work on that no one else wants to do."

"That's not entirely true, Scott. Don't forget, you're one of the new boys on the block. It takes time before the big jobs get filtered down to you."

I was a little taken aback. With some hesitation I shrugged my shoulders and said, "Well?"

"You don't want to rock the boat, Scotty." Steve gave me an encouraging nod. "Anyway, it *is* time that you started on a project of your own. "

"Great! When?"

"Give me a couple of days, okay?"

"Sure."

"We'll need you to attend several product orientation meetings in August."

"Okay. Anything you say, Steve." I was ready to fly. My own project! I didn't even notice until later that I had just agreed to more training, the very thing I had been complaining about.

Steve got up and walked around the desk. As he passed by the window he motioned for me to come over. "Looky here," he said, pointing down to the street. "New recruits."

I looked down. It wasn't so long ago that I had been down there, full of hopes and ideals, and confident of my future. It was a strange feeling looking at them now. Chills washed over me. It felt as if something had been stolen from me.

Chapter 5

THE CHOICE

I did exceptionally well on the project Steve arranged for me. In return, I got a larger project. As I finished them, the projects came more often, with greater time limitations and fewer resources to accomplish them. Things were definitely on the move.

Well into my second year at CSC, I found myself accepted by my peers, my supervisors and managers. Kama was the only person with whom I didn't mesh well. She had been promoted to supervisor of New Products. Kama was still a thorn in my side but of all the girls I dated or was friendly with, Kama was the only one who could get to me. For some reason I liked her for that.

We were both dedicated. However, I found Kama's loyalty toward the company questionable. Her level of energy and the quality of her work, on the other hand, were unmatched by any of her peers. She had an outstanding employment record. Kama had smarts— and the fresh mouth to go with it.

As for myself, well, I wasn't rocking the boat as Kama was, but I was steadfast and loyal. I can't recall one incident when I didn't put the company first. Not one.

It was a clear Saturday night and the crisp Atlanta breeze sent a chill through me. My stomach churned with nervous anticipation. My boss's boss was hosting an invitation-only gathering. for selected employees. Worse yet, the senior execs would be watching each of us and taking notes.

I parked my car in the neighboring church parking lot, as the invitation had instructed. During the brief walk to the door, my eyes took in the lavishness of Atlanta's wealthy. I felt honored to be invited. Some day I'd be living in a mansion like this, I told myself.

The black-tie event was a first for me, and probably for most of the others in my group. The rented tux straightened my spine and put a touch of Hollywood in my soul. New shoes and a fresh haircut added to my confidence. As I walked, I noticed a few couples. It hadn't occurred to me to bring someone.

The mansion was more than beautiful. A brilliant white, it perched majestically high off the roadway with at least two acres of well-groomed landscaping around it. The front columns were like those seen in Rome and were at least twenty feet tall. The wide stone stairs were built for royalty. The grounds were lit with multicolored garden lamps.

This opportunity was too good to be true. Here I was, about to greet the executives of CSC, the decision-makers of my future. I was determined to act my best to show them how much I wanted to become one of them.

I recalled the phrase, "Welcome to the men's hut," that I had read about in my last management class in college. The Men's Hut was an anthropological term describing a ritual where tribal leaders required young males to endure death-defying feats in order to attain true status as a warrior.

These rituals also exist in our everyday business cultures but any injuries are psychological rather than physical. Nonetheless, this evening was my formal acceptance into the corporate palace. It was my initiation, so to speak.

As I approached the front steps, my stomach became queasy and my palms began to sweat. At the top of the royal steps, I leaned a hand against a column, took a deep breath, and got a smear of white cement paint on my palm for my efforts. I looked around. Where could I wipe it off? I'd forgotten a handkerchief. Then I noticed that the columns were not imported from Rome, or even made of stone. They were plain concrete, poured into a form, and then painted to match the mansion.

Just as I was ready to grab the lion-headed door knocker with my clean hand, a servant opened the door, bowed, and gestured for me to come into the foyer. Sheepishly I held out the paint-smeared hand and he handed me a tissue. Then he directed me to the main reception room. Each footstep on the marble tile brought me closer to my fantasies of wealth and reinforced my desire to work as hard as I could.

"Hello, Scott." I heard someone say behind me. I turned to see Ed Vernan. I was totally unprepared to see him and felt awkward. I quickly stuck my formerly painted hand in my pocket in case any traces of paint remained. "Ah ... hi, sir."

"Welcome. Glad you could make it tonight."

His grin was pronounced. Unlike Ira Eastman, who was short and stubby, Vernan was lean and tall. His narrow, usually tense face reminded me of a war hero who has seen much combat. Vernan looked tough and his voice reverberated power.

He looked at me cheerfully. "I've heard a lot of good things about you, Mr. Hendrick."

"Thank you." Nervously, I looked at my shoes and saw a scuff. "Great party, Mr. Vernan."

"Why, thank you."

A strange look overtook his face and he backed up a step. I wondered if he was trying to figure out the basis for my instant party evaluation. It was a foolish statement. I wasn't even past the entrance foyer yet.

"Where's your date?"

That rattled me. "I thought it might be better to come alone. That is, to prevent any complications."

Vernan narrowed his gray eyes. "Complications?"

"You know what I mean, Mr. Vernan."

"I'm not quite sure I do, Scott."

My bowels lurched and threatened to let loose. After a couple of moments of silence, the executive V.P. concluded his talent search with me and said, "Anyway, enjoy the party, Scott."

My thoughts ran crazy. Did I blow my career? So much for the Men's Hut and I hadn't even entered the damned party yet!

I grew angry and felt as if I had to challenge Vernan in order to regain his confidence in me.

I walked over to the wet bar. The bartender, probably a moonlighting college student, asked, "What will you have, sir?"

I was still pent up, full of steam, and feeling nasty. "Give me a gin and tonic. And don't forget the damn lime!"

He didn't appreciate my tone. He muttered, "Stupid bastard," as he poured the drink. Setting the drink in front of me, he quite innocently said, "Excuse me, sir. Did you say lemon or lime?"

I was furious. "I said lime, not lemon!" Now I really felt like a jerk. "How much?" I asked, extending a five-dollar bill in his direction.

He looked at me as if I were from another planet. "It's on the house."

I paid for my arrogance by relinquishing the fiver. "Here, take this, kid. You deserve it."

He took it and slid it in his vest pocket. He nodded his head in appreciation, despite my nasty treatment.

So far I had screwed up in the foyer and at the wet bar. I found my way to the terrace, which overlooked the manicured garden, thinking I couldn't possibly screw up there. At first I didn't see Mark Sloan and his beautiful fiancée, Lynn, standing off to the right as I came out. Mark was the youngest and most recently appointed manager at CSC. I had a major distaste for him, mainly because of his rapid advancement and his uncanny ability to brown nose his way to the top, a political strategy I detested.

My anger was dispelled by an irresistible urge to stare at Mark's fiancée. While sipping my drink, my eyes caught hers. I had seen many beautiful women in Atlanta, but Lynn took first prize. Standing in the moonlight, she was a goddess in human form. She offered a magnificent flirt by way of a dazzling smile and a wink. I was just about to take another sip then and my arm shook as I raised the glass to my lips. I missed my mouth and spilled some of the drink down the front of my tux. She knew exactly the effect she was having on me and held eye contact with me. Despite the spilled drink, I smiled in return. The exchange continued, as though somehow we touched each other from a distance. I warmed to the game. Who cared about Mark? I wanted to go to her, but held back. Maybe there would be a better chance later.

The evening had given me back something. Once again I felt worthy. Cautiously, I managed to slip away and get another drink. I was careful not to disturb the college kid this time. He gave me a damp bar rag to wipe off my tux with. As I was handing the rag back, Kama sidled up to me.

"Well? Are you going to buy me a drink or what?"

"Hi, Kama. Sure, I'll buy. What's your pleasure?"

With a naughty look on her face she said, "You!"

"Ah ... how many drinks have you had, Kama?"

"Th-r-ee-e." The way she said it rhymed with whee.

"Maybe you've had enough."

"Damn it, Scott. I'm putting the make on you."

"Yeah, I can see that."

"I don't know why I'm crazy about you. Maybe it's your tall slender body and lovable face."

"Well, uh ..."

"Maybe it's because we're so different. I know I can't get serious with you."

"That's not necessarily true, Kama."

"Maybe it's because I like to tease you and make you angry."

"Now you're getting hot."

"That's right!" she said, rubbing her body suggestively against mine. Then she giggled and whispered in my ear. "I am hot!"

We were interrupted by Ira Eastman. "Hello, Scott. Hello, Kama. Are you folks having fun?"

We both laughed awkwardly, nodding our heads like children with a secret.

"I didn't know you two were dating each other."

"She's not my date, sir. I came alone."

Kama looked at me with remorse. Ira looked at Kama and asked, "Who did you come with?"

"No one, Ira."

"You're kidding. A beautiful girl like you, alone?"

Then Ira turned to me and said, "Scott, I'm surprised at you." His face grew more intense, as if I had hurt one of his children. "You don't know a good thing when you see it."

That was a definite kick in my ass.

"How can you let a little girl like Kama slip right through your fingers? How can you not desire a beautiful girl like her?"

I didn't know what to say, so I shrugged my shoulders and grinned. Ira grinned back but displeasure tainted his face. "Well," he said, "I hope you two get to know each other a little better. Try to have some fun tonight." He left abruptly.

What a mess. Kama wanted sex and I wanted success. Ira wanted to be paternal. This reception was getting too heavy for me to cope with.

"Damn you, Scott! How can you not get screwed and yet get screwed at the same time? What's wrong with you?" Kama shouted in frustration.

I reddened, took her arm, and dragged her back to the terrace where there was more privacy. I was mad and as I pointed my finger at her, she began to cry. I stood there like an idiot. I didn't even have a handkerchief to offer her.

We sat down on a sculpted stone bench. Neither of us spoke for few minutes.

"Scott, I was serious back at the bar. Ever since you and I met at the employee indoctrination, I've had some feelings for you but you're always cold to me. I became more infatuated with you than I thought possible. I wanted to get close to you. I wanted to love you but each time I made an attempt to reach you, you found a way to turn it into an argument or a joke. Well, I don't need you or your macho bullshit crap!"

"I'm sor—"

"Listen," she said, cutting me off. "I felt that you were an honest and genuine person but your brain is always caught up in its ego-centered self. You constantly talk about becoming a vice president at CSC. Why do you punish yourself so much? I never see you have any fun."

"Success is my ambition, Kama. I'll have fun when I reach the top."

"Well, put some reality into your ambition. Live life successfully each day. Don't put your life on hold for the future," she said, wiping a tear away.

"Reaching for vice president is my way of having fun."

"You're just fantasizing, Scott. Reality is all around you, except in your head." She patted her hair to make sure it was in place, wiped her cheeks free of mascara with the palms of her hands, and said, "It's time for me to go."

I sat there alone for five minutes and realized that nothing I did was right. I felt like a shithead. My only salvation was to get Ed Vernan and Kama out of my mind.

Remembering Lynn's magnificent flirtation was the only bright light shining in my life.

Chapter 6

GO GET 'EM, TIGER!

Three weeks later John Mayes gave a sensational speech at the company's annual New Year's Kick-Off Celebration. I was awed by his ability to inspire me. He emphatically invited us to join him in the pursuit of the world market share.

His closing message grabbed me right where I live. "The key to CSC's success is its people, without whom there wouldn't be an excellent product or the opportunity for success. For all of you who are listening in earnest, give me your talent and your spirit and I'll give you the opportunity to climb the corporate ladder faster than any other company. Go get 'em, tiger!"

Go get 'em tiger! kept ringing over and over in my head. It became the focus that eventually led me to become even more self-centered, ambitious, and protective of my time.

Once the formal presentations were over, the crowd of employees migrated into the Grand Ballroom for the reception banquet. Tom McClane and his wife approached me. "Hi, Scott," Tom said, "I'd like you to meet my beautiful wife, Cheri."

"I'm pleased to meet you, Cheri."

"Nice to meet you, too, Scott. Tom has told me some interesting stories about you."

"I guess he has a few good ones up his sleeve." We all grinned. Then, still full of the hype in Mayes' fabulous speech, I said, "John Mayes really said some heavy stuff tonight, didn't he?"

Cheri looked at me curiously. "May I ask what Mayes said that was so important to you, Scott?"

"Basically, he said me that if I work diligently and consistently hard for the company, some day I'll be on top, just like him."

"I've heard that before. Tom fed me that line ten years ago, too," Cheri said.

"Yeah, but did you really understand what Mayes actually said? To get to the top, you gotta have spirit and believe in the company. You know, go for it all."

"Aha," Cheri said softly. Then she spoke a bit louder. "All that 'go get 'em, tiger' crap again." Her face twisted with contempt.

I was not about to let my vision be tarnished by a woman I'd just met. Though we were both uncomfortable with the conversation, I felt obliged to stand up for my beliefs. "Well," I said, "I can see myself as a vice president and I know I can get there, no matter how hard it is, or how long it takes."

Tom became frustrated with me and a bit defensive. He took his wife's hand. "Say, Scott," he said, "I've worked extremely hard to get to this position, but there's one thing I won't do: give up my soul to a corporation. Not for money, fame, or success. It's too damn ridiculous to think hard work alone can make you successful. Besides, it takes knowing the right people and saying the right things to them, something you need to work at real hard, my friend."

Before Tom and Cheri moved away, I had seen pity for me in their eyes. I stood there alone, my mind racing. I re-ran the conversation with my boss and his wife. They weren't too impressed with me tonight, nor was I. My head numb with confusion, I stood motionless, like a deer caught in headlights. Time didn't exist.

Why had Tom said that about his soul? What is a soul, anyway? Did I even have one? And if I did, why would CSC want it? I was confused. Was I supposed to react? Why not fight for the top? What's wrong with wanting to be a vice president?

"Hey, big fella! Are you posing for a sculptor?"

I turned around and there she was, within arm's reach. Lynn.

"Are you all right, Scott?"

My head was still spinning with unanswered questions, but I got my eyes to focus on Lynn, and what I saw took my breath away. Her body was slender and her peach gown was stunning. My conversation with Tom and Cheri evaporated. My heart pounded as the blood rushed wildly about my body.

"I'm Lynn," she said.

"Er...yes, I know. How...how did you know my name?"

"I have my sources." She gave me a brilliant smile.

I took a deep breath and managed to ask, "Like to dance?"

"A little later, maybe," she hinted.

With Lynn just a few inches away, and oozing sexual energy all over me, I was getting aroused. She stepped back to judge my bulging vulnerability. "Catch you later, Scott. I don't think you can walk too far in that condition."

I watched Lynn go. Each step, each move, each heartbeat was recorded somewhere deep in my being. It seemed as though it took an hour for her to walk into the crowd. My pulse began to normalize. My thoughts returned but I found myself in a curious dilemma. I wanted Lynn. What's more, in that moment, I wanted her even more than I wanted the vice presidency. I'd never experienced this before.

What the hell did "Go get 'em, tiger" really mean, anyway?

Chapter 7

TAKE THE HILL

L ater that year, several major events occurred in my life. Work-wise, I finally got my wish: a national assignment. It definitely was a biggie. I was to go to each of CSC's twelve regional offices to give demos of our new product. This meant unquestionable visibility, potential big-time raises, and some down-to-earth power. I would be "the guy from head office." I had finally arrived.

The other main event was my marriage to Lynn. She swept me off my feet. We had a small chapel wedding, with her parents and a few friends. Even my mom and dad flew down for the day.

Our first three months together were something out of a movie. I was infatuated by Lynn's beauty. Like other Southern belles, Lynn was gorgeous. She stood five-ten and was sculptured to perfection. Her long, wavy hair reached down to her mid-back and she tantalized the hell out of me. Lynn had style. She was sharp, intelligent, and professional. She could have been with anyone she chose, and she chose me.

In my temporary insanity, I put CSC on the back burner during our courtship. However, what I saw as the responsibilities of marriage brought me to my senses. I was also exhausted from her sexual drive. She wanted to make love two or three times a day and I constantly had to come up with new excuses.

Lynn was an unbelievable person. Determined, straightforward, sharp, witty yet compassionate, Lynn had an edge over most other women. She had to be outstanding in order to survive the harshness and demands of her job. Not many people can handle being the supervising nurse in charge of an emergency room.

We purchased a house in the suburbs, one I had always dreamed of having. Occasional visits to church and some gardening on Sundays were about the most I could squeeze in for myself to enjoy. Between my projects and Lynn, I found little, if any, time to do anything else. I'd had no religious background growing up and only attended church because Lynn wanted me to. I didn't believe in the hellfire and damnation I'd heard other people talk about off and on in my life. I didn't know anything about a soul. I didn't even know if I believed in God. I'd heard too much about a vengeful God from the TV evangelists. I don't know what I believed in, except myself.

Despite Lynn's vigorous sexual appetite, I managed to drag myself into the office before eight each day. Generally, I tended to stay at the office late, maybe more often than I should have. And coming home exhausted let me off the hook with Lynn. Lynn, on the other hand, worked just as hard, but she always managed to have dinner ready by 6:30 and still be ready for a "quickie" before we ate.

It was 4:30 on a Friday afternoon when the phone in my office rang. "Scott," Lynn said, "let's go to the movies tonight."

"I'd like that very much, sweetheart. What do you have in mind?"

"Is Scarlet and Rhett okay with you?"

"Not again, Lynn! We've seen that several times."

"But it's romantic!"

"Naw! How about going out for a bite? Something different. Thai food maybe, and then decide."

"Well, that sounds good, too."

She sounded down. I wondered what was up. "Hey, Lynn. What's up?

"Nothing, I had a very rough day at work and a lot of aggravation on top of it. I just don't feel like going home and cooking. I want to be pampered, I guess."

"Sure."

"I'll pick you up at six, then."

There was a gentle knock on my office door. As I looked up, I saw a woman's leg stretching slowly out from behind the doorway. Knowing it was Lynn's, I moved to intercept it. She grabbed me by the doorway and began kissing me. The evening was off to a wonderful start.

At a little Thai restaurant, Lynn managed to have a few more drinks than she could handle, causing us to cut our evening short and head for home. Lynn was acting strange; she seemed sad or depressed. As I pulled into the driveway, she grabbed the keys from the ignition and demanded that I make love to her in the car. I was tired and just wanted to go to sleep. And I didn't want the neighbors to see us making out like two kids in the back seat in front of our own home.

We went inside and she seemed to feel better within a few minutes. Resting her head in my lap, I asked her if everything was okay but she remained silent.

She got up to make some coffee and I followed her into the kitchen. "Sweetheart," I said, "is something bothering you?"

"There are a lot of things bothering me."

"Let's hear them."

"How come you're so kind to me tonight?"

"What do you mean?"

"Lately, it seems that all you're trying to do is avoid me. Is that true?"

"A little. Maybe there's too much sex, Lynn."

She looked at me as though I'd wounded her deeply. "I didn't want to hear that, Scott. I love making love to you. I am so attracted to you it hurts. You're still my big, handsome, fun-loving guy with enthusiasm, dreams, and courage."

She began to cry. I didn't know what to say or do, other than change the subject. "How's the job?"

"It sucks, too!" she cried.

I was beginning to feel like a therapist. "Come on, Lynn. What can I say to help you?"

"I feel as if you're slowly slipping away, Scott. Like you're forgetting me by devoting all your thoughts and energy to your work."

"That's true. To some extent, anyway."

"Are you being honest or stupid?"

I couldn't tolerate being called stupid. I could feel my anger rising. "Hey, wait just a minute! I love my job. I work for a great company. I have potential. I don't need a wife to drag me down!"

"I don't believe what I'm hearing!" she cried in frustration and disbelief.

A chill enveloped us. I didn't understand her or what she was trying to say. Our beautiful evening together had come to an abrupt end.

One night, about a week later, I walked into the house after nine o'clock. "I'm home, sweetheart!" I shouted.

"No shit! Where the hell were you?"

"What do you mean, where was I?"

"That's exactly what I'm asking you, Scott."

"At work. I had to finish up some important business."

"Listen, mister, I worked all day, too. I cooked supper for two people—you and me—and I hate eating alone. I hate you for throwing your life away over a silly job that you think is going to make you a vice president! Why do you want to be a vice president anyway? Go on, tell me."

"I don't know. It's just a goal I have." Why *was* I stuck on vice president?

"Well, why not shoot for the top? Why not go for president?"

"Damn it, Lynn, you've got your nerve. I love my job. I'm proud of it and I don't like it when you belittle all my hard work!"

"Well, why can't you at least give me a call?"

I was speechless.

"We've been through this before," Lynn said evenly but firmly.

"I promise. From now on I'll call you. Okay?"

But as the months rolled by, my work schedule grew even more strenuous. Traveling two to four days per week became part of the initiation, to test my loyalty to the Men's Hut. Lynn became increasingly cold and distant, and complained at length about my absences. She also complained that my health and attitude were deteriorating by traveling around the country in tightly packed airplanes.

On weekends, I sought the comforts of home and the necessities of life. She, on the other hand, wanted to go out and be romantic but I'd had enough of the restaurant scene, hotels, and desperate people. She'd had enough of loneliness and I just wanted to be left alone. The tension led to sporadic, mechanical lovemaking that left us both unsatisfied.

As our lives continued in this vein, Lynn grew weary of me and of our relationship. We were in our mid-twenties, both earning good wages but spending them very foolishly on furniture and expensive electronic equipment to ease the pain.

Our home life continued to deteriorate. We grew increasingly distant with each other. Every time I arrived home from a few days of travel, the atmosphere became more strained. But the worst was yet to come. I had received new orders from McClane and had trouble finding the courage to tell Lynn.

Late one Saturday evening, I walked into the living room with two mugs of decaff. I'd prepared for this all week and now it was the time to drop the corporate bomb on Lynn's head.

"Sweetheart, I've got some good news and some not-so-good news to tell you," I said in a most wimpish way.

"Well, let's hear the bad news first and get it out of the way."

"Ah … Let me tell you the good news first, darling."

"Whatever," she said with a shrug.

"I've been promoted to Regional Coordinator of my project." My eyes lit up with the hope of congratulations from Lynn.

"That's great, Scott. Does that mean you're going to get a raise, too?"

"No, not yet." I downplayed that particular pain and embarrassment.

"Oh! So that's the bad news?"

"Uh-huh. That's not all of it, Lynn. I'll have to install my new programs at each regional office site and train the staff on the systems."

Lynn's face made Mt. St. Helens seem peaceful. She knew exactly what my assignment meant. With a cold voice she asked, "How long at each site?"

"Five to six weeks each."

"And how many regions?"

"Twelve," I said with remorse.

"Twelve! That's over a year's worth of traveling away from home!"

"I know, I know. But it will go quickly."

"Damn it, Scott!" Tears brewed in her eyes.

"Listen, Lynn. This is my big opportunity to *prove* myself."

She got up and walked around the sofa. Tears streamed down her face. She grabbed a tissue and looked at me as if I was a lost and pitiful puppy. "Prove what to whom? Not to me, Scott! I can't take you being away so much as it is. Not another year of this! I don't believe this is happening to us, and I don't like it one bit!" She shook her head, "I'm sorry for you, Scott."

"But, Lynn, you don't under—"

"I do understand! If my husband had a job in which he was respected and compensated for it, then fine. I could manage him taking on some travel and a few long days at the office. At least I'd know he was growing and had the confidence of the company behind him. But those bastards are using you.

"Do you think I enjoy seeing you come off those stupid airplanes, burnt out and exhausted? I *hate* seeing you like that! You're being used, my friend. When I first saw you, you had confidence and drive. Now you roam around, hoping to get recognized by kissing the behind of anyone you think will pay attention to you.

"Let's face facts, Scott. Your ambitions and the company's desires don't match. You work your ass off for the company and they cash in on it. You've told me this yourself many times.

"Listen to yourself for once, Scott. Learn from this. Don't keep going on, thinking and hoping that someday they will send you to the top. They're stealing your soul, sucking us both dry. And you're letting them."

Holding a handful of tissues and looking totally defeated, she said softly, "I'm going to bed. And one more thing. I don't feel like having you next to me tonight."

Chapter 8

TWO PINTS OF BLOOD, PLEASE

I spent the next few days telling myself that Lynn was over reacting. Everyone knew there was a price to pay if you wanted to get to the top. Asking her to wait just a few years wasn't unreasonable. Then we could be happy. So I buckled down even harder to prove to her that I could make it. The job easily consumed twelve hours a day at the office. My extensive travels also put an extra burden to my health. I was stressed out. Lynn's faithful attempts to "put some sense into me" only got pushed into my subconscious. I kept hearing her in the background, pleading with me to get a better job. I wanted the challenge I already had and found myself locked into my job even more.

While this was going on, and without any conscious planning on my part, my beautiful, lonely but distant wife got pregnant. This was a major shock to me since we had agreed to avoid conception. I didn't know if I should celebrate or try to get Lynn to abort it. Who needs a kid anyway?

Lynn was furious about my attitude and totally dismayed at my lack of compassion for her and the child to be born. But in her fifth month of pregnancy, Lynn got me close enough to feel the fetus move. When I felt the first kick my heart melted and I accepted her pregnancy. This gave Lynn new hope for me and I treated her as a special person during this precious time for mothers-to-be.

Like everything Lynn did, childbirth went without a hitch. The new arrival, Richard, was named after Lynn's father. He was a healthy infant and always in Lynn's arms. Having Richard around created a family for me that I really didn't want, but babies are cute. Anyway, Lynn did most of the baby stuff.

As I saw it, Lynn had her baby and that should take her attention off me. My job was demanding, and that's what was expected of me. I valued my position at CSC and never let go of my drive for corporate recognition, although many times I felt guilty over the way I placed my job ahead of the needs of my family.

Knowing that Lynn would have her hands full with the baby was a relief for me. I knew that I had a role in nurturing Richard, but he was here for her, not for me. I didn't need him; I was too young to be a father. Things would be better for Richard and I when he grew up. We'd do many father and son things together and we would make up for lost time once I had succeeded at CSC.

One Monday night I awoke all sweaty from a frightening dream. The corporate jet I was traveling in was going down. I heard myself calling out to Lynn, "I don't want to die! My life is incomplete!" My love for my family glowed brilliantly as the plane tumbled through the air making a deadly and horrific sound. My last thought was that I wished I had told her I loved her before I left on that trip.

When I awoke that Tuesday morning, I felt shitty. The day before had gone too fast. It was one of those 8:00 a.m. to 9:00 p.m. "stretch" days. I was scheduled for a brief trip to Dallas on Wednesday but I felt as though I had contracted the bubonic plague or something. I was limp and exhausted. My stomach felt like an overripe honeydew: mushy, slimy, and decaying. Richard began to cry and Lynn leaped out of bed. It felt as though the God I didn't know had abandoned me.

As I lay beneath the sheets, thoughts raced willy-nilly through my head. I was flooded with guilt about work, Lynn, our son, my health, and my life. I felt trapped, torn between my ambition for the vice president's position and what it was doing to me and my family. Did I really die in that plane crash? Was my subconscious trying to tell me something?

"Scott, get up. It's 7:30. You're late!"

I peeked out from behind the sheets and instantly took pity upon myself. "Sweetheart, get me a couple of aspirins will you? Please?"

"What's up, Scott?" she asked coldly.

"I'm sick as a dog."

"I knew sooner or later you'd break down from all that work." Feeling attacked, a surge of defensive energy shot through me. "Damn it, Lynn, a man can get sick once in a while! Why do you always have to blame it on my job?"

"Take these, they're stronger. Maybe they'll knock you out for the whole day."

"I can't do that. I've got to prep for the Dallas trip."

Lynn put her hand on my forehead. "You're running a fever." I looked into her face the way I had done with my mother when I was a child. "But I need to contact the office."

"Like hell you're going to work—today *or* tomorrow. I'll call in sick for you."

"Get off it, Lynn. I'll do my job; you take care of the kid."

"The kid?" she snapped. "You mean the boy named Richard—your son, whom you don't even know?" Lynn began to cry and left the room, slamming the door behind her.

I didn't take the pills she had brought me. Instead, I got up and called the office. I committed myself to the Dallas trip.

Later that day, I managed to raise my aching body out of bed. I acted better than I felt to impress Lynn. I moved slowly towards the kitchen. As I strained and shoved the four-hundred pound kitchen door open, I saw Lynn and Richard babbling to each other in toddler talk. The moment she saw me, Lynn sympathetically volunteered, "Let me make you some good old-fashioned chicken soup."

"Naw. I'd like a bologna and Swiss, with mustard and ketchup."

"That's not going to help you or your stomach, Scott."

"I don't want any stupid soup. You sound just like my mother."

"Well screw you! I suppose you're heading out for Dallas tomorrow, too."

"Yep. I feel fine."

"Bullshit!"

There was a brief moment of silence between us.

"What are you doing home, today? Do you have the day off?" I asked.

"No. I don't have the day off. I called in sick because of you!"

"Oh get off it, Lynn."

"Damn it, Scott. You got me very upset this morning. And Richard, too."

"No, I didn't."

"I have a demanding job, too. All the nurses are thinking about going on strike for more pay and respect. Supervising the emergency room is extremely difficult, mister. I'm under a lot of tension between administration and the nurses. But you never care about my work, do you? You don't even care about your son."

"Who in the hell do you think you are, talking to me like that?" I yelled.

"In your hat, Scott. The truth hurts, doesn't it?"

The quarrel grew more intense. Ancient shards of unsettled grudges surfaced as verbal ammunition. Insult after insult was hurled without regard to effect.

Richard was off to one side, propped up in his highchair by cushions. He burst into a wailing protest against the exchange taking place before him. I turned to look at him. For a moment everything froze. My mind went blank. What was he crying about? And then it came to me. The child was terrified by the hostility between his only sources of love. I'd seen my parents act that way too often. I had vowed never to repeat what my parents had done to each other. It suddenly occurred to me that their parenting had prepared me more for marital combat than for expressions of love.

Lynn grabbed Richard and stormed off to the bedroom. I slumped down at the kitchen table in a daze.

What was I supposed to do? My marriage was one long argument; my fatherhood an empty biological fact, the result of a careless accident. I was alone, in a horrendous conflict about who I truly was.

Then I heard an inner voice say, "It's time get help, Scott."

I could see the company counselor, but suppose my boss or my peers at CSC found out. That would be just too embarrassing. No, I'm going to tough this one out myself, I resolved to myself.

Chapter 9

SCRATCH ONE EMPLOYEE

C arol came into my office looking lost. As she approached my desk, I could see she was troubled.
"What's up, Carol?"

"Did you hear about Kama?"

I could tell it must be serious so I got up, pushed the door
shut, and invited Carol to sit down. "So, what's going on?"

"I think Kama's leaving CSC."

"That doesn't surprise me."

"I mean, I think she was asked to leave."

I sat forward on the edge of my chair. "What do you
mean?"

"Please don't tell anybody. I just need to tell someone who
is close to Kama."

"I won't repeat anything to anybody, I promise."

"Last week, Ira Eastman called Kama into his office. About
ten minutes later, she came out looking pissed-off. She rushed
past my desk muttering, 'This shit-ass place doesn't understand anything!' "

"What do you think she was referring to, Carol?"

"I didn't know then, but I do now. You know Mark Sloan
and all his bullshit, don't you?"

"Please, don't remind me of Mark Sloan."

"Well, he told Ira that Kama spoke negatively about him at
a business meeting with two clients from Gant Foods. Ira believed Mark and called Kama into his office to reprimand her."

"Was there any truth to it?"

"Ira asked me to call Mr. Presley at Gant to apologize for
Kama. Presley told me that Kama hadn't really said anything

bad. In fact, he was annoyed by Mark running to Ira with a bunch of lies."

"So what did you tell Ira?"

"I began to tell Ira that Mr. Presley, being polite, accepted the apology. But when I told Ira that Presley was pissed at Mark, Ira lost it. He didn't let me finish. He defended himself and made disparaging remarks about Kama in front of me."

"What about Sloan?"

"During the whole week, that bastard kept telling Ira negative and exaggerated crap about Kama."

"What did Kama do?"

"Nothing. As far as I know, she went back to work in her usual spirited way."

I listened and realized that brown-nose Sloan had scored another victory. He had done this before when he felt threatened by others. On the sneak, he'd slowly and methodically feed a negative image of an innocent employee to Ira, who always swallowed it whole. Sloan became Ira's informer and he went up another step on the corporate ladder.

"What should I do, Scott?"

Lost in my own thoughts, it took me a moment to re-connect with Carol. "Did you tell Kama anything?"

"Not yet."

"This has really gotten you down hasn't it, Carol?"

"Kama's innocent and I screwed up by not telling Ira exactly what Mr. Presley told me. And that Sloan is lying."

"Hmmm."

While Carol waited for guidance, I searched for answers. Kama was officially on Ira's shit-list because of Sloan's insecurities and hostile tactics. Ira's ego was threatened and needed protection. His insecurities and selfish quest for power erased any concern for others or for the corporation. Kama was being sacrificed on the alter of personal power, and I didn't have a clue what to do.

"Well, Scott?"

I was lost for an answer, troubled about the proper thing to do, and dumbfounded by why Ira would let his need for power damage productivity by terminating Kama. I was also fearful about possible implications for myself if Ira ever found out that I knew anything. Filled with doubt, I said, "I need to think on this overnight. I'll ask Lynn what she would recommend, since she's into organizational management at the hospital."

The look on Carol's face told me she wondered whether coming to me for guidance had been a mistake.

"Carol, I'll get back with you tomorrow, first thing. Okay?"

She stood up. "Please, Scott, I feel real bad about what I did. Kama could get fired because of all this crap. I need help."

I didn't like Carol's news. I was confused and disgusted. How could Sloan do such a despicable thing? Kama was the best person on the team. Without her, we would fall behind with our schedule.

That night I asked Lynn's opinion. After hearing the facts, she told me a few facts of life regarding CSC. She said her old fiancée was very egocentric and he hated Kama with a passion. Even when Lynn had been involved with Mark, he had feared that Kama's success would interfere with his relationship with Ira. Mark had told Lynn that Ira liked people who saw things his way, right or wrong, and that he would lie to Ira just to please him. Lynn had already known that Kama was not going to last long with CSC due to the fact that Kama had little tolerance for corporate games and office politics. Lynn believed that leaving CSC would be the best thing that could happen to Kama.

Lynn's explanations were accurate and helpful, but made me feel on edge about my position and career at CSC. Could I become a target just like Kama? And did I want to devote my life to an organization that would allow ruthless men like Ira to destroy a beautiful free spirit like Kama?

When I got to my office the next morning, there was a sealed envelope on my desk from Kama. She wanted me to meet her in the cafeteria at 9:00 a.m. sharp. She knew that Carol had spoken to me.

I bought two black coffees and sat by the corner window. Kama came in a moment later and headed toward me. She was as beautiful as ever in her three-piece suit. Full of zest, she grabbed a chair and sat down.

"Shit, Scotty. I popped the old fucker!"

"What?" I was strangely annoyed.

"I got myself fired! Today's my last day."

"Oh no, Kama!"

"Yeah. The old buzzard offered me the opportunity to resign gracefully."

"I don't understand."

"Look, Scott. You know how I once felt about you."

"Yeah, but—"

"Despite our differences, we've managed to keep up a friendship. We've shared some good trade secrets, haven't we?"

"We sure have, Kama."

"Well, I did something foolish. I let shit-head Sloan get too close and he saw me as a threat so he pulled the knife on me. Do you know what I mean?"

"Lynn's been trying to tell me about that stuff." I was uncomfortable with what Kama said, but I sensed a lot of truth in what she was telling me.

"Wake up, Scott. It could happen to you, too. Look, Sloan told Ira a lie about me, knowing all the time that Ira would buy into it."

"What do you mean?"

"Remember how we used to fight about company bureaucracy and corporate games? Well, Ira always had his concerns about me. I found that out through Carol and a few others."

"But why? What did you do?"

"He couldn't figure out if I was loyal to him and his cause. He didn't trust me."

"But didn't you get great increases and promotions?"

"Sure I did, but each time he gave them to me, he kept pumping me up to excel and excel some more to get the job done."

"So?"

"He also told me that I was too high-spirited and that my behavior was not acceptable."

"You're joking!"

"No, I'm not. He said I was arrogant and that I had to prove my loyalty to the company. I've had several arguments with him in the past six months."

"You can't tell your boss what to do, Kama. He'll feel that you're out of place and disrespectful."

"I guess so, Scott. But when a man's values—his greed for money and increased profits—interferes with my values of health and life, then we are at an impasse."

"But you can work that out."

"Not when Sloan tells Ira that I think Ira's a bottom-line, greedy slave driver."

"Is that what Mark said?"

"Worse. Ira feels that I betrayed him so he wants me out."

"Can't you explain the truth to him?"

"It's over. He's made up his mind; he's labeled me. And Sloan just moves one step closer to the vice presidency."

I was sad when Kama said that. I saw how enormously unfair it was. My own anger toward Sloan bubbled to the surface. It was as though I were caught in a combat zone, where lies and deceit did battle with truth and hard work.

"I want to say good-bye, Scott. Give Lynn my best, and Richard, too. Tell Carol not to worry; I understand her predicament. And if you see Sloan, piss on him for me."

Kama looked as though she wanted to cry. She left as quickly as she had arrived. I argued with myself that Ira must have had his reasons for what he did, but Kama was his best supervisor. I didn't understand. I couldn't put two and two together.

My inner voice kept trying to tell me something but I couldn't make sense of it. Was there a message for me to decipher? I felt like a mule sitting on my ass: helpless not knowing what's happening around me. Had my big ears gathered enough information to learn from this mess? Or was I going to keep carrying the corporate bullshit on my back all the way to the bank?

Chapter 10

MR. MENTOR

In June, I received the company's prestigious five-year pin. It commemorated all the determination, aches, pains, and joy that had brought me to this point in my career. To celebrate the occasion, I took Lynn out for a special dinner at her favorite restaurant, Don Pablo's.

"Let me toast to our success, sweetheart," I said, lifting my wine glass.

While the glasses clinked together, Lynn added her own toast: "To our family and happiness."

She kept peering into my eyes. A second clink punctuated Lynn's desire for me to be more of a husband to her and a father to Richard. Family was at the top of her list.

Dinner was delightful. Treats like this were long overdue. As the meal progressed, I noticed Lynn had that special expression on her face. She looked sexy. I loved to see her tease and taunt me in her erotic moods. She still had the same magnetic power to draw me to her as she had when I first saw her out on the balcony at Ed Vernan's mansion. I felt so good with her at that moment that nothing entered my thoughts except making love to her. She knew me well, and knew just how to touch me and excite me.

The waiter politely interrupted. "Your espresso, *Signorina.*"

Lynn looked up to thank him. As she turned, the low neckline of her dress draped even lower. That weakened my ability to concentrate on anything except my beautiful and romantic wife. I was counting the moments. Time was the only thing that stood between us.

"I haven't seen you feeling like this in a long time," she said to me.

"Neither have I. It's amazing how much we forget how wonderful these moments are. We let them slip by us until they no longer exist."

"You need a lot more of these good feelings, Scott, if you want to survive and be happy."

A feeling of humility rippled through me. I looked into her eyes. "I know. What you're saying is true."

We sipped our coffee and enjoyed looking at each other with honest, open faces. I felt at peace, although still quite horny. Then Lynn's face lit up a bit. "Maybe you should ease up at work, Scott."

"I still believe that some day real soon, I'll get recognized for all my hard work." Then I crossed the line again. "Do you know what it means to me to become a vice president?"

Earthquakes don't happen in Atlanta but I suddenly felt one. "No, Scott, I don't. I *do* know that you have put so much of yourself into your job and don't have much to show for it. If you put *one-tenth* of all that effort into your family, you would be closer to Richard and me—and a lot happier, too."

I wasn't enjoying the turn things had taken. It could become another gripe session and I didn't want to ruin the beautiful dinner or lose that special feeling I had for Lynn. Not tonight. I sat there for a few seconds and didn't say a word as I waited for the shock waves to subside. My inner voice ricocheted inside my skull.

Face it, Scott. Have you ever had a better time than with Lynn? Answer: I haven't.

When was the last time you got a hard-on at the dinner table? Answer: Never.

Is what Lynn said about your job true? Answer: Very accurate. Richard is three and I don't even know what his favorite TV program is. I'm also getting fat and sloppy.

"Scotty. Scotty!"

I came out of my trance and saw her beautiful face watching me with tender concern. I realized how truly powerful she was.

"Scott, all I can honestly say is that your job *owns* you. It seems to me that you don't actually love your work but rather you're infatuated with your ambition to become a vice president. It may do some good to get some feedback from your friends at work.

"Remember Kama? She was always trying to reach you. I often thought she was in love with you but she's gone and probably very happy that she left. Ask a few people. Call your dad in New York. Maybe he can shed some light on the situation."

"Yeah, right," I scoffed.

"All I know is that you need some different perspectives and some balance, Scott. There's one thing I can definitely share with you: it's really beginning to hurt, watching you being consumed by your job and not having you with your family."

The next day at the office, I did some serious soul searching. Lynn had finally reached deep enough inside of me to get me to examine my work values. That wonderful dinner at Don Pablo's was important to me.

I kept thinking about the vice president's position. Actually, I was ego-tripping on the fame, glory, and power it would bring. Was it because I still had to prove something to my parents? To myself? Was I that insecure? One day I hated CSC and the next day I was turned on by the damn place.

I wore the corporation's prestigious pin religiously. Whenever I took off my suit jacket, I'd stick the pin in my tie. After a while, most of my silk beauties had pin-holes in them and had to be permanently retired to the tie rack. But that pin was alive. That little silver sucker sometimes had the power of a ball and chain, especially the days I was stressed out and overworked. Many times, while flying to regional offices on my precious weekends, or feeling the pain of being away from Lynn and Richard, I hated the stupid thing. My loyalties were in some kind of ping-pong tournament.

On the ping side, I enjoyed the prestige the pin reflected. It meant that I was associated with a well-known and successful corporation. Membership had its privileges. As I grew more confident at work, success and acceptance became more comfortable.

On the pong side, there was the pain of loneliness and family separation, especially when leaving to go on a business trip. Sometimes I stared at my naked body in a hotel room mirror and felt depressed and devoid of romance. The worst mental knockers occurred whenever I traveled through a big city airport and felt like an animal herded up and down ramps, dreading being stuffed into a flying, aluminum tube.

My mood oscillated, and the ping-pong tournaments became more frequent. Well into my fifth year at CSC, my values were in flux. I was undergoing change. Each week brought me different sensations. Sometimes my mind ascended into the hierarchy of the corporate suite— confident, successful, and accepted. But when this brought only hollow and infrequent praise descending from above, I became quite confused in my role and with my place.

And then it happened. The long awaited event arrived. McClane walked into my office one afternoon with an excited and cheerful face.

"Hey, Scott, I've got some great news for you."

"Yeah? What's up?"

"You've been nominated to attend the next CSC Management Development Program."

"What? Really?"

"I got the word late yesterday."

Recognition. The moment I had been waiting for. The permanent dwellers of the Men's Hut must have awakened to my talents, hard work, and loyalty. It was gratifying to know that my career and executive potential were taking a more definite course.

The program was sponsored by the Human Resources Department and designed by the fine folks in Training and Development. The purpose of the program was to groom potential corporate management personnel. The training group had implemented the first Management Development Program last year and planned to do another program each September.

After Tom let his news sink in, he offered an important caveat. "Remember, Scott, this is only a nomination. We won't be getting the final word until August first."

"What are my chances for official acceptance?"

"You're ninety-five percent in, unless something major happens."

"Like what?"

"Like a major fuck-up! Just remember, there are no guarantees. One thing is for sure, though. There's lots of training and hard work planned for the participants."

"Don't worry about that, Tom."

"Well, I've got to head for a meeting. Congratulations!" he said upon leaving my office.

The moment had finally arrived. All the hardships, trials, and frustrations I had endured over the past five years evaporated. This was it! I was elated and couldn't wait to tell Lynn the good news. I called but there was no answer. I left a message for her to call me.

I needed to share my excitement with someone. Doug? Steve? Roger? Kama? Yeah, Kama! I searched my database for her number. She'd moved back to California.

A young female answered cheerfully. "Good morning! Shasta Computer Systems. May I help you?"

"It's not morning. It's one-thirty in the afternoon," I laughed.

"Not in California."

"Oh, yeah. I forget that you're three hours behind us here in the East."

"Fortunately, we're usually three years ahead of you folks in the East," she quipped.

I felt like snapping back at her, but I was too excited to let anybody interfere with my good news. "I'd like to speak to Kama Rowley, please."

"Just one moment, I'll connect you."

Kama sounded as fantastic as ever when she came on the line.

"I've got to share some great news with you, Kama. But first, how are you doing and what's happening with you?"

"I'm so glad you remembered me. I actually miss you, you know."

I was instantly honored and flattered. I picked up on a few other buried feelings, too. I didn't know what to say, so I just mumbled, "Yeah, me, too."

"How's Lynn? Are you still married? And how's your son?"

"He's growing up fast. Thanks to Lynn, I've finally been able to spend more time with him."

"Are you still busting your balls at the shit-house?"

I was reluctant to say yes. "Yeah, same old place."

"So you still haven't learned anything," Kama said without emotion.

I didn't want to challenge her because I knew she had bad feelings for the place, but I thought she might like to share my excitement. "Kama, I called to tell you I've been nominated to CSC's new Management Development Program."

"Oh. Congratulations." There wasn't much enthusiasm in her voice. I was taken aback.

"Well, Scott, it sounds like you've given CSC your all and things are working out well for you there."

"Yes. I finally feel appreciated for all my hard work."

"I hope so. You've worked your ass off for those guys. Is Carol still there?"

"No. She left about three months after you did."

"What happened?"

"She couldn't take anymore of Ira and the way he used people. Remember your friend Mark Sloan?"

"That asshole."

"Well, Sloan and Ira got to be real buddies and Carol couldn't tolerate all the crap taking place in Ira's office. One day she came in and said to me, 'Those two idiots are at it again. They found someone else to kill.' "

"Poor sweet thing. She really got upset about my termination, didn't she?"

"You were her idol, Kama. She spoke about you and your values as 'a most progressive woman.' She respected your honesty and sincerity."

"We were friendly, but I never thought she saw me that way. Do you know what she's doing now?"

"She went back to finish college. As a matter of fact, she's out your way at some environmental program at the University of Washington."

"Can you get more info for me? I'd like to call her."

"I'll get a number for you."

"Well, Scotty, it feels like old times — you deeply involved with your job and me waiting for you to say something romantic. It's all kind of funny now, you know?"

"Funny?"

"Here I am, for some strange reason, talking to a man whose work values I detest, but to whom I used to be attracted."

I wasn't sure how to take that, so I changed the subject. "So, what are you doing these days, Kama?"

"After I left CSC's extortion racket, I took a long vacation. Actually, it was a retreat, so to speak. I went on camping trips, did some white-water rafting, did lots of hiking and skiing in the Sierras, bought a mountain bike and joined a biking club. My body looks great. You ought to see it—ha!"

"I'd like to."

"Do I hear a change in you, Scott? You wouldn't say anything so bold before."

"Well, I guess I'm becoming wiser these days."

"Then why are you still at CSC?"

"Because I finally see signs of a corporate promotion."

"Scott, I left CSC and landed a great job out here, greater than you can imagine."

"After leaving CSC the way you did?"

"Scotty, you must always grow from setbacks. I saved a few bucks to take a couple of months off and enjoyed myself. I got mentally and physically healthy, wrote up a new resume, put a new smile on my face, and felt very optimistic about who I was.

"My third interview was great. I was offered thirty-five percent more money than CSC paid me. Scotty, that's like a seven-year salary increase in just two months! I even get some stock benefits after one year of service."

My mind went into a spin during Kama's career update. My mental and physical health were stretched to exhaustion. There was pain on my face when I smiled because it was usually so rigid and tense. Could Kama be right? Never had I thought it possible to quit a job the way she had and come up smelling of roses.

"So, what exactly do you do, Kama?"

"I work as a technical consultant for a new computer company called Shasta."

"What does a technical consultant do?"

"My job is similar to the stuff that Tom McClane and Doug do at CSC, but I do it at client sites. I customize our systems to match their needs."

"Heck, that's what I do at our regional offices."

"Scotty, they even gave me a company car and a corporate credit card."

"What the hell am I doing working for peanuts?"

"No, Scotty. You're working for people who use you, who squeeze all your energy and creativity from you, who consume your hopes and dreams and then turn them into their own profits."

"You're still bitter about Ira, aren't you, Kama?"

"Yes and no, Scott. Let's face it: He lost and I won. At that time, it seemed that I was the bad guy and he was the righteous one. But he wasn't thinking about CSC. He was thinking about himself, about his precious ego, and his delicate insecurities.

"When I first started at Shasta, one of the senior managers who hired me acted very similar to Ira. Her name was Pamela Limer. This stocky little powerhouse treated me like gold because she saw me as an asset. Unfortunately, her aggressive and manipulative political positioning became too apparent."

"I don't get it."

"Now that I think of it, that whole scenario reminds me of the one I had at CSC, only just the opposite."

"What do you mean?"

Kama thought for a moment and then said, "The bitch told our corporate vice president that I was too assertive with clients, that in order to consummate a sale, I gave away the house. Well, Cindy Gayner, my V.P., took me out to dinner one night and opened up to me. She wanted to get to know me better. Follow?"

"Yeah, sure."

"I remember specifically a question Cindy asked me about integrity relating to customer satisfaction. Then she asked me if I knew how Pamela perceived me as a technical consultant. I told her that Pamela tells me that I'm doing exactly what she would be doing if she had my job. As a matter of fact, she said being assertive with the customer is healthy and bending a little to make a sale is sensible.

"Well, it didn't take Gayner too long to figure out the scheme of things and the true color of Pamela. She got her walking papers about two weeks later. The V.P. believed in consistency, integrity, and honest straight talk. She despises bullshit and condescending remarks about other people. That's exactly the trap Pamela fell into with Gayner. Score one big one for me."

"Yow! You're always getting in strange predicaments."

"Hey, Scotty. If you never venture beyond your little shell, then the world outside doesn't exist for you. You'll live an egghead and die an egghead. If you break through that shell, you might get eaten by an unfriendly monster—or you might find out that you're not an egghead and learn to enjoy your new world."

"You make a lot of sense, Kama."

"I had fun talking to you, Scotty."

"How are the guys out there?" I asked.

"I get enough dates. There's one guy I like a lot. He has his own Tai Chi Chuan studio and is doing quite well as a journalist, too. We're doing a lot of environmental things together."

"Tah Cheek Won? What's that?"

"It's ... Scotty, I'll send you some literature, okay?"

I looked at my watch and realized that I had to meet Tom in five minutes. "Wow, Kama, we've been talking for an hour. I don't believe how fast time flies when we're enjoying ourselves."

"Hey, Scotty, do you know Ben Roberts at CSC? He's in the Training and Development Department."

"Yeah. I hear he's pretty far out with his ideas."

"He's their senior trainer and knows his stuff. Ben is one of the few people who can really make you think. He's a great guy—and a great lover, too."

"Kama!"

"Listen, my friend, let's keep in touch. Say hello to Lynn and the folks at CSC. And send me Carol's number."

"Will do."

"And, Scotty? Do get in touch with Ben. He can truly shed some light on things for you. And one more thing ... Scotty. I still love you."

There was a moment of silence. Then I heard a click and the dial tone.

"It's official," McClane said. "Fretman called about an hour ago and gave me the confirmation. You're officially in, my friend."

Tom leaned back in his big black manager's chair and gave me a paternalistic look. He tapped his desk with a zany-looking red-cased lead pencil and said, "Scott, remember the night when you first met my wife, Cheri? Well, she always asks how you're doing. I guess you were young and naive then and she has this maternal thing, you know?"

"I remember her well. She really snapped at me."

"She sure did. Anyway, I mentioned your nomination to her last night and she suggested that I speak to you about a few things."

"Okay."

"I've been thinking about your career path, Scott, and would like to suggest that you keep your desire to become a corporate executive more of a secret."

"Why? Surely it's good to speak up and express your goals."

"That's fine for kids and entrepreneurs but when you're in the corporate environment, or any business for that matter, you may easily threaten someone who is power hungry. I've seen it happen many times before at CSC. Whenever an innocent and assertive individual discloses his or her plans, some turkey who's protecting his turf counterattacks."

"Hmm. I've just heard the same from Kama."

"How is she?"

"She's fine and really doing well. She said to say hello to you and the rest of the group."

"Now that's one fine girl."

"Why are you telling me to be cautious, Tom?"

"You've been here over five years now and have only marginally gained from all your hard work."

"You can say that again!"

"I've supported you. Believe me, I have. But somehow, you just don't get the right type of visibility. Grant Fretman asked me to remind you of a few things as well."

"Like what?"

"Well, it's better if I quote him directly. He said, 'Tell Mr. Hendrick not to expound on how he's carrying CSC on his back, like a mule would. He's got to learn that other people cringe when they hear that self-pitying talk.' "

"What the hell is he talking about?"

"Just listen for a minute, Scotty. Fretman's a V.P. He's also a puppet-type so when he says something like that, it probably came from Ira or Ed. Am I making myself clear?"

"So I shouldn't act like a mule?"

"Right."

On the way back to my office, I stopped to get a drink of water from the fountain near my office. My emotions were playing ping-pong again. Damn it, every time something great happened, something shitty happened, too. Just then, the water spurted out of the fountain and drenched my new silk tie. My mood was darkened by thoughts of incompetent maintenance people and the impossibility of getting a drink of water without getting soaked.

I heard my phone ring so I shook the excess water off the tie and bolted into my office. Out of breath, I heard an unfamiliar voice on the other end of the line.

"Hi, Scott. This is Ben Roberts. Your friend Kama just called and asked if I would do her a favor."

"Oh, she did, huh?" I was suddenly hit with a twinge of jealousy.

"Would you like to get together tomorrow for lunch?"

I held myself in check for a second, thought about it, and said, "What the hell! Sure! Can you give me an idea of what this is all about?"

"Well, Scott, it's about our friend Kama, but it's also something about the Management Development Program. How's eleven-thirty at Los Rajas?"

"Sounds good to me," I answered.

Chapter 11

FATHER TO SON

The rush for Mexican food in Atlanta hits its high right at noon. Getting a table early is essential. I got to Los Rajas just before eleven-thirty and quickly secured my favorite outside table. The view was excellent. There were plenty of trees and lovely ladies to help relax the nerves.

I took the liberty of ordering two beers to greet the arrival of Kama's secret friend. After a few sips, a tall, bearded man with an exceptionally athletic physique approached the table. Resting his hands on the chair's back he said, "By chance, are you Scott?"

I looked up at him. "Ben?"

I grabbed a beer and pushed it over to him. "I hope you like beer."

"Beer's not one of my favorites," Ben replied, "but I'll have this one." He lifted the golden brown bottle and saluted me with it. The ease with which he did this simple thing impressed me. Ben looked like he would be comfortable anywhere—the bridge of a ship, an airplane cockpit, or chairing a board meeting. So what was he doing at CSC, and why was he having lunch with me, I wondered.

After a few minutes of talking with Ben, I realized that he was not in the least way threatening to me. He was distinctively sincere, attentive, and caring. For someone in a corporate position at CSC, he was quite unusual. I began to open up to him, which was quite unusual for me.

We spoke briefly about Kama, both exchanging kind words about her. Then Ben leaned a bit forward, looked directly at me and said, "So, Scott, why are we here?"

That took me by surprise, but actually I knew why. With a bit of hesitation, I moved myself forward and replied, "I need a little insight on what's happening with me at CSC. Maybe you can tell me about the Management Development Program."

"Let's get to know each other," he said, "before we get into any serious dialogue."

"That's fine with me, but how do we go about it?"

"We need to talk and meet often to share our experiences."

The food we'd ordered arrived. I accepted that Ben knew what he was talking about and that he had the expertise to go with it. I needed an extra second or two to keep up with his thinking. Eating is a good buffer when discussing sensitive matters, especially when they relate to the workplace.

While eating his enchilada, Ben said, "Congratulations, Scott, on being accepted to the MD Program. You'll do just fine in it as long as you can balance your job, your family, and the program."

I wasn't used to hearing compliments and I appreciated the positive reinforcement. "Thanks Ben. I know I'll do great."

"But you might be in for a big surprise, Scott," he warned. "The program is two-sided, you know."

No, I didn't know. I thought about it out for a moment. "Well, doesn't everything have two sides?"

"Scott, do you know why they want you in this program?"

"Sure do. They want to give me the opportunity to excel and become a member of their team." He looked reassured, as though he was reading my thoughts. I attempted to express my knowledge of the corporate process. "You know—the Men's Hut."

"The Men's Hut indeed," said Ben. "I haven't heard that expression in years." He thought intently for a moment. "Scott, I need your full attention on this if we are to get anywhere. Can we work on that?"

I searched for a rebuttal, feeling pinned against the wall and deeply scrutinized. "What do you mean, Ben?"

"Simply this. I have an excellent high-paying job at CSC. I do a few things for the company and I do a few things for the employee. I have a mission in life that I'm going to share with you. It's based on three facts. Successful corporations thrive on successful people, successful people also thrive on successful corporations, and each contributes to the other's growth. My self-appointed mission is to make sure that those three aspects materialize. Unfortunately, I'm finding that mission to be close to impossible. When the corporation and employee can no longer serve each other, the proper thing to do is to encourage a mutual and beneficial separation."

"That sounds like textbook stuff," I said.

"But it's not written, Scott. Instead, what really takes place is that the corporation and the employee fail to communicate their expectations, needs, and resources. In turn, one or the other attacks or withdraws and the work relationship falters."

"Like what happened to Kama?"

"Not exactly, Scott. Kama was the victim of office politics, the power game."

"That's what she called it, too."

"Call it what you like, the real issue is that corporations are made up of people. People run corporations. Eventually the most powerful people, generally speaking, rise to the top and use the people below them for their own purposes, not necessarily for the corporation's benefit."

"I'm trying to understand what you're saying, Ben. But why do you call your job 'a mission'?"

"Scott, I'm idealistic. I'd like to see the gap between corporate management and the employees become nonexistent. But in reality, I find that my job serves the needs of the corporation more than those of the employees. If I like my job and want to keep the paychecks coming in, I'm forced to serve the corporation."

"That sounds contradictory."

"Not quite. I'm here with you to prove it. Right now, I'm doing what I feel is right and beneficial for you, the employee. I make an effort to help as many people at CSC as possible. That's what motivates me — helping others grow. There's a bit of danger involved, too. I'm taking a risk because it can get back to the wrong person and easily become distorted.

"What I'm trying to do within the framework of my position, Scott, is close the gap. I survive day by day by offering valuable information to corporate management and to the employees. Over time, I may see some success. I truly believe that the employees want to do a better job and that the corporations are beginning to open up and encourage that process. By no means do I see this happening rapidly."

Los Rajas would be a great place for the United Nations to open a world forum. Ben and I spent two full hours grappling with some serious concepts. We agreed to meet the next day to continue building a friendly relationship.

When I arrived back at the office, there were ten messages waiting for me. Lynn had called from work twice. I called her immediately.

"Hi, sweetheart," I began cheerfully.

"Scott, Richard is sick. The nursery called and we have to go get him. I can't get away from work until five-thirty. Can you get him?"

I really wanted to say no, but I agreed to go. I packed a few items in my attaché case and sped off to get the little guy.

At the nursery, a very attractive woman was in the small lobby, waiting to get her child. She wore a sexy white halter top with a plunging neckline. Her denim shorts were quite short and her long legs were beautifully tanned. I found it difficult not to look at her. An elderly aide came out carrying her daughter and holding Richard's hand. Apparently both children had slight fevers.

"Here we go, Ms. Peters. Christy's feeling down and out. She's been crying a lot."

Richard came running over to me and jumped up into my arms. We spoke baby babble for a moment, then he put his head on my shoulder and closed his eyes. It was good to hold him that way.

I couldn't take my eyes off Ms. Peters. I realized that she was reciprocating my interest. Caught off guard, I felt her eyes connect with mine. A sexual tingle permeated my body. We stared at each other, despite our children's needs. I truly enjoyed the rush it gave me.

Standing like an adolescent child in love waiting for a chaperone, I foolishly walked closer to her and said, "Looks like your daughter needs her momma."

"Hi, I'm Ginger Peters," she said. "It's great to see a father pick up his child at the nursery. I wish I had a husband to come and get his daughter."

"You're too beautiful not to have a husband," I blurted out and instantly regretted it. That was a line a school kid would have used.

"Are you married?"

"Yes, I am," I sputtered, as if I were ashamed of my marriage.

Ginger's sapphire eyes, warm and uninhibited, looked into mine. With her child snuggled in her arms, she said, "You're just the kind of guy I could love."

That knocked me back a foot or two, and it was hard not to think of Ginger for the rest of the evening.

At ten o'clock the next morning, I met with Ben in his office. As agreed, I brought the coffee. The decor was eclectic, reflecting Ben's collection of Ansel Adams photographs and paintings of sacred landscapes. The Indian and tribal artifacts scattered throughout the room reminded me of the omnipotent natural order of things. Ben's body and presence exemplified health and innate harmony.

He stood at least six feet tall and had broad shoulders and a trim waistline. He exuded an air of confidence.

"We've got about one hour today, Scott."

"What do you know about the Management Development Program, Ben?"

"What do you want to know?"

"Can it help me achieve a vice presidency?"

"Of what company?"

"Come on, Ben. Stop kidding around."

"Seriously, Scott. What company?"

"CSC!"

"You're serious, aren't you?"

"Very."

"What's so special about CSC?"

"It's a great company. I feel I can make an important contribution to its success."

"Bullshit, Scott. Please don't be offended, but it appears to me that what you really want is fame and recognition. Isn't that the answer?"

"Sort of. But I believe I can serve the company as a V.P."

"Suppose you get promoted to the vice president's position. What policy and programs would you implement?"

"The first thing I'd do is get rid of a few people. Then I would—"

"Hold on, my friend. The first thing is to learn about the position is its assets, its liabilities, its resources. Who are the good guys and who are the bad guys."

"Yeah. I see what you mean."

"If and when you get promoted to any corporate level position, Scott, it's because someone higher up wants you there. You will already have been playing their game for a while and have proved yourself in that capacity."

"What do you think I've been doing for the last five years? Every day I'm proving myself by working ten, sometimes twelve, hours a day, going to all kinds of training, serving the company with all my energy and loyalty. And you say that I *still* must prove myself?"

"Yep. And prove, and prove, and prove. It never ends, Scott. If the guy on top of you wants you to sell your soul for the company goal—well then, what's your price?"

"Didn't they nominate me for the Management Development Program? Aren't they saying I'm in?"

"What they're saying upstairs aligns to their needs more than yours. You definitely have proved that you can do the work, but whether or not you have the character or personality to fit in with the boys at the top is another matter. They're testing whether you can play their game and jump on their command."

"I've done that already!" I was exasperated.

"How well do you know Ira Eastman?"

"Well enough."

"Well enough tells me nothing, Scott."

"Well enough to know that he wants me to work long hard hours if I want to get to the top."

"That's obvious, Scott. But what are his likes and dislikes? What are his hot buttons? Those are the things you need to know. How can you get to know someone if you avoid establishing a relationship with them? You must take a chance and see what the relationship yields."

"You mean like Kama did?"

"Precisely! After a while Kama and Ira found themselves in a very familiar scenario. Regardless of Kama's hard work and demonstrated loyalty, the relationship fell short because of the conflicting personalities within it. Soon, no matter how well Kama performed, Ira would want her out. He would feel either threatened or incapable of manipulating her values and her behavior. Either way, the relationship was doomed."

"But I think Ira's great!"

"Well, then, how do you think Ira perceives you? And no guesses!"

I pondered that one and kept coming up with blanks. What Ben was saying bothered me deep down inside. "Listen, Ben. I think I've had enough of this subject for one day. I need to get back and catch up on my projects, if that's okay with you."

Ben looked at me with sadness. He got up and walked over to me and said, "You're due for a break, Scott. Let's not forget what we discussed. I've learned a lot from you this morning, and I hope you have learned something from me as well."

The days progressed and work piled up. And there was plenty to do to prepare for the Management Development Program. It was to start in three weeks and would last nine months. Since I had to work long days, I felt it wise to negotiate some child care arrangements with Lynn. Initially, she got pissed off when I told her about my anticipated workload but when I offered to pick up Richard on Mondays, Wednesdays, and Fridays, it turned out well for everybody. Lynn could relax and not have to drive so far to pick up Richard every day.

Richard and I saw more of each other and I arrived at work early each day and stayed late only a couple of days. Needless to say, Ginger and I saw more of each other and the chemistry between us grew, especially when it came to values and her willingness to listen to me.

At three o'clock one Friday afternoon all hell broke loose in the office. CSC's stock price had dropped drastically from $110 to $43 per share, a major financial loss for its stockholders. Somehow news got out that CSC's cash flow was unhealthy and that a buyout was possible. As a result, two bulletins were released from Corporate Finance. One reinforced the capital strength of the company while the other emphasized that higher profits and lower production costs would improve our company's position in the market. Therefore salaries would be frozen for the next six months.

Tom and Doug were outside my office debating the memos. I decided to join them. "You guys look like hell froze over," I joked.

Doug looked at me as if he wanted to kill me. "Shut up, shithead! I've just lost eleven thousand dollars and you come out here making jokes," he snarled. I hated his macho attitude. "Pretty smug, aren't you, Scott? Just because you had nothing invested in the company doesn't mean you don't have anything to lose."

"Cool it, Doug," Tom cautioned. He didn't look well, either.

Like a jerk, I asked Tom how much he had lost.

"Still want to become the next vice president of CSC, Scott?" Tom asked.

I was just about to nod, when Tom lost his composure. "Does twenty-seven thousand bucks mean anything to you?"

I definitely nodded.

"That's what I lost today," Tom snarled, "So why don't you go upstairs to Ed Vernan, the guy who hates the sight of you, and tell him to step down because you're going to be the new executive vice president!"

Blood rushed to my face so fast it hurt. My stomach knotted and I felt like taking a crap. Tom and Doug looked at me with disgust.

"Listen, shithead," Doug hissed, "you're not a corporate mule, you're worse! You're a total corporate fuck-up!"

My face flamed scarlet as I tried to compose myself but the attempt was futile. I managed to retreat into my office and slam the door.

As soon as the coast was clear, I got myself out of there. For the first that I could recall, CSC had become distasteful. It was full of egotistical, snarling, white-collar jackasses. Everything was falling apart. All that hard work, loyalty, and sacrifice was gone. All because the faceless, uncaring, self-serving stockholders in New York decided to sell out. Now my goddamn future was going right down the drain. At least my money was safe.

Depressed and filled with self-pity, I stewed in my anger as I drove to the nursery. When I pulled up, Ginger was just getting out of her convertible. My eyes carressed her long bare legs as she slid out from behind the wheel.

I walked in front of her car. For a moment, everything was bliss. "Hi, Ginger."

"Scott! What a coincidence."

Ginger stood so close to me that I could feel her body heat. An animal sexuality came up in me that wanted to rip her few clothes off and take her on the hood of her car. And the look in her eyes told me that she probably wouldn't object. I needed that boost to shake off the effects of the office massacre. Without missing a beat, I said, "If you have the time, let's treat ourselves to a cold beer before we pick up the kids."

There was no hesitation on her part so we drove off in her car.

At a nearby tavern, we chatted for about an hour about our jobs and our lives. We sat close to each other in the booth, and my hand brushed her breast at one point, sending a shock wave through both of us. Ginger was quite free in her touching me as well, and I loved it when she would put her hand on my knee while she talked. We were definately falling in lust. She easily calmed me down and made me feel comfortable, something that Lynn didn't seem able to do lately. Above all, her sapphire eyes and the Southern accent captured me. She had simple values. She didn't expect much and lived a simple day-by-day life. I envied her.

Saturday morning meant relaxation. Staying in bed was one of the few respites life offered to most hard-working idiots like me. I dreamed that I was at an executive board meeting. Ed Vernan and Ira Eastman were yelling vulgarities at each other. The press was frantically knocking at my door, trying to get in for interviews. I was the new CEO. I also wore a large blue diaper. Each side of the diaper was secured by a Velcro tab with the CSC logo on it.

The company had gone bankrupt because Ira had placed an advertisement in *Mother Earth News* for eight million dollars. The copy suggested that CSC would save the world from the greenhouse effect by designing the first anti-ozone software. Apparently the scam wasn't well received and our stock crashed. Ira had told the press that it was my idea and I was ready to kill him.

While I was still deeply immersed in the dream, Richard's soft little foot poked at my throat. He had apparently walked into the bedroom and climbed in bed with me. Still dreaming about Ira, I jumped and yelled out, "Kill the bastard!" Richard began screaming. Lynn rushed into the room.

"What the hell is going on?" she yelled.

I grabbed Richard to comfort him, but Lynn must have thought that I was trying to strangle him. Her face livid, she snatched Richard from my arms. It wasn't a pretty scene. I froze and shut my mouth. Lynn stormed out of the room with Richard in her arms.

Alone in our bedroom, I was bewildered. Maybe I am a shithead. Everybody calls me a mule. Who am I, anyway? Where am I going? I lay in a cold sweat. Only the thought of Ginger calmed me.

Richard trotted back into the room and climbed under the sheets next to me. Once again, his foot knocked against my face. I saw his innocence. I kissed his precious little foot and chuckled. Richard snuggled against me and fell asleep.

Why did Richard come back? He wasn't afraid like his mother was. Maybe he could tell me a few things about life that I needed to know. Children possess that special gift of simplicity. Did he come back to comfort me?

I longed to hold him close to me and tell him that I loved him but I didn't know how. I looked at his sleeping face. "How can I be a father to you when I never learned from my father?" I whispered. I leaned over and kissed his forehead and hoped Richard would somehow know what I was talking about.

I mulled over the dream I'd just had. How had I ever permitted Ira to place that ad anyway? Obviously he had tried to put one past me and make me look like a fool. Vernan had been shouting one phrase at me, over and over. That one phase I couldn't recall seemed to be the key to the dream.

And why had I been wearing a diaper?

Chapter 12

Truth or Consequences

A voidance was going to be the in thing for me for the next few weeks. Doug and Tom blew off some pent-up steam towards me. Ben left me alone. Richard lifted my spirits. Ironically, it was the little guy who kept the father-son relationship going. Lynn thought I was becoming manic-depressive. I was happy one day, sad the next. A lot had to do with how recently I had seen Ginger. Her warm smiles and casual touches reassured me that I was an okay guy. I needed that.

On Wednesday morning, Doug called and asked if he could see me right away. "Why?" I asked. "You don't need an invitation."

"Hey, Scott," he said humbly as he walked in. "I'd like to apologize for the comments I made to you last Friday."

I should have kept my cool but instead of accepting his apology, I shouted, "You ought to be sorry!"

Doug's body tensed, as if he was a linebacker ready to engage in a scrimmage. Then he backed off. "I'm sorry. Okay?"

"Yeah, okay." I really didn't want to let him off, but I didn't feel like a fight. Without another word, Doug left and I suddenly felt empty and desolate.

I called Ben.

"Sure," Ben said, when I asked for a meeting. "Let's meet in half an hour."

I felt better already. Talking to Ben did wonders for my depression.

Ben's confident, relaxed face was a welcome sight. Politely, he asked about my weekend. I brushed his question off with a joke.

"Well, Scott," he asked, "what's on the agenda for today?"

"For starters, what's the purpose of the Management Development Program?"

Ben brought his hand to his face and sighed. "Sometimes I really wonder." Then he chuckled.

"Come on, Ben! Let me in on the real scoop."

"The real scoop, huh? At CSC, it's really a career-path requirement, which simply means that you have to go through it if you want any kind of decent promotion. It doesn't have too much to do with becoming a V.P. or any other corporate position, unless you excel substantially beyond the rest of the class and have the same chemistry as the boys at the top.

"On the other hand, if you do poorly in the program—which is negative visibility—then you might as well pack it in. Your best bet is to do the best you can and keep your ears and eyes open."

"That sounds strange to me, Ben. Isn't the program intended to groom potential managers and corporate staff?"

"On the surface, yes." Ben gave me a troubled look. "But CSC uses the program differently from what most employees believe. The guys at the top make a big deal about who they nominate. Next, they crank up the importance the program plays in one's success at CSC. The program participants push themselves to exhaustion, like it's a boot camp. And finally, senior management expects you to be even more dedicated and committed upon graduation."

"I don't get it."

"Regardless of where you work," Ben said, getting up and walking to the window, "all corporations have their own personality. Some are autocratic. You know, military stuff—top down, do what you're told. Then there are companies that fall into a more benevolent category: 'We listen to and like our employees but we, the corporation, are the boss and the bottom line is that profits take priority over employees, the community, and the planet.' Back in the sixties and seventies, most corporations fell into this group.

"As we move into the next century, we're going to find more changes in senior management personalities and policies.

There's a good chance that corporations will put more emphasis on their employees and the environment. This new social awareness advocates improved quality of life and respect for the planet's environment."

"So where does CSC belong?" I asked.

"It's generally benevolent. With the exception of several VPs, I feel the company will eventually lean toward more employee integration and participation."

"That's good, isn't it?"

"Yeah, Scott, but as of today, CSC is dominated by a few VPs who are very dictatorial. They practice top-down fear tactics with the people under them and, needless to say, with the rest of the organization. They are the power people and they have great influence on most corporate matters.

"For the most part, the staff and management of CSC are a great bunch of hard-working and fun-loving people. But to move up into the ranks beyond middle management is like climbing Mount Everest."

I was beginning to see situations and circumstances I hadn't seen before. Maybe it was because of what Kama had shown to me before. I still wanted a better answer about the purpose of the program. "Ben, please be more specific. Is the MD Program going to help me get to the vice presidency?"

I waited patiently for about fifteen seconds while Ben appeared to be gathering his thoughts.

"No, Scott. I'm sorry. It is not going to help you—not with Ed Vernan and Ira sitting up there. Sorry, kid."

I closed my eyes and felt as though my soul had abandoned me. I wanted so much to become part of the company and its goals. The players in the picture Ben had just painted were like giant Cyclops and I was just a slave mule carrying their wealth to the castle high up in the mountains.

Suddenly my thoughts took on a life of their own. Without warning, my reality shifted. I felt dizzy, as though I were leaving my body. I tried to stop it but that only accelerated the process.

I traveled swiftly through a tunnel. It seemed like forever before I saw a light at the end of it. The light got brighter and brighter until a luminescent lady appeared. I couldn't make out her features but I knew she smiled at me. I felt it with all of my being. Then just as suddenly as she had appeared, she disappeared and I was traveling backwards through the tunnel. Then everything faded to black.

"Scott! Scott! Are you all right?" Ben was shaking me.

I opened my eyes and saw concern on Ben's face. I had no idea how long I had been daydreaming or what I might have said. I felt strangely peaceful.

For the rest of the week, I worked steadfastly to complete as many projects as I could. Over and over in my mind I tried to remember the daydream I had in Ben's office.

I picked up the business section of the Sunday *Atlanta-Journal* and read about last week's blow to CSC. It said that CSC's stock had "flattened out" near the bottom and that the profit outlook was bleak. *Profit!* That's the word that had been nagging me from my diaper dream. Now I'd gotten it.

I remembered Ed Vernan sarcastically yelling down to me, *"Profits, mule. Profits, mule. Profits speak louder than people!"*

I began to lose some of the motivation needed to carry me through the long, hard day's work at the office. My energy level dropped and a mild case of depression shut down any desire I might have had to look beyond the hour. The weekend looked bleak, too. Lynn wanted to go on a picnic at the lake but I hated summer picnics, with the bugs and noisy kids. Worse yet, I had to read a thick business management book over the weekend to prepare for the MD Program.

The weekend looked depressing.

Ginger and I met prior to going to the nursery. It was becoming a standard practice for us to meet in the tavern and have a drink or two together before picking up the children. She maintained her charm, definitely boosted my ego, and actively sought my companionship. Her flirting had become downright provocative. She had taken to removing my tie when we would meet, saying I didn't need to fly the corporate flag when I was with her. Each time she took my tie off, however, her hands would stroke my chest a little more and she would look up into my eyes with an invitation that was hard to ignore. In fact, many times I almost didn't ignore it, but the thought of what that would do to Lynn made me pull back.

"Is there any chance that you and I can get together this weekend, Scott?"

That was the first time she'd spoken what her body was telling me, and I was infatuated with the idea. But again, guilt and remorse overwhelmed me. As if I were engulfed by molten lava, my mind screamed, *I CAN'T DO THAT!* If Lynn even finds out that I came here with Ginger, I'll be up shit creek.

Depression flooded over me. I was pulled between my wife and the woman I wanted to be with and, quite frankly, confused and lost. But I knew what I'd better *not* do!

The weekend was just as lousy as the business book I was trying to read. The picnic was a major blunder. Between the biting bugs and Lynn's constant nagging to quit my job, I felt like sinking to the bottom of the lake. I even entertained the idea of going off to be with Ginger. She, at least, thought that I had a great and exciting job.

It was déjà vu the following Monday morning. The warm muggy rain slowed traffic down, and inside their cars, young women put finishing touches on their makeup and hair, preparing to face their day at work. For me, the exhilaration of going to work was gone completely. Six years ago, nothing could have bothered me. Today, just the sight of the damn office building knotted my gut.

Most of the people in the elevator were soaking wet. The smell of damp clothing and newspapers added to my misery. Maria was now married with three children and thirty extra pounds padded her frame. Her barely disguised sex drive and candid come-on mannerisms were even worse than the first day I saw her. I didn't understand how Ira tolerated her in that position, but she had to be doing something right. He always joked around with her and seemed to enjoy her the way she was. I wondered what hold she had over him.

Just as I got to my office, the phone rang. Tom wanted to see me right away. On my way down to his office, I encountered Maria with her mouth full of cookies. I gave her my usual hello.

"How's Ginger, Scotty?" she taunted.

I froze. How did she know about Ginger? "Who?" I gulped, trying to hide my fear.

Maria leaned suggestively across her desk and looked at me. "You know who I'm talking about." She wore that "insider" expression when she had some particularly juicy gossip to impart.

"Not really," I croaked. My voice had taken on the quaver of a teenager who had just gotten caught with his hand up his girlfriend's skirt.

"Ginger. The one who called here a few times asking about you," Maria said with a smirk on her face.

I was saved from having to reply by Tom calling to me from his office doorway. "Come on, Scott!"

Thank God! "Yeah, right away!" I hurried off to Tom's office, grateful for the reprieve.

Tom was impatient when I entered his office. "I need a favor from you."

"Yeah, sure! Go ahead."

"Do you know Sam Hawkins?"

"You mean the old guy who does the Unix programming?"

"Right. Well, he's slated to retire next year and I'd like you to take over some of his more important projects for me."

"I don't like to do Unix programming, Tom."

"Yeah, I know, but we all need to pick up our share."

"Why can't we just hire somebody to replace him?"

"Not a chance with the salary freeze. There's no way that I would even suggest a new requisition to Ira at this time. He'd never forget that move."

"Come on, Tom. Are you afraid of Ira?"

"No, Scott. I'm just not stupid enough to talk about spending money when Ira wants to hear about savings. So forget that idea."

"How about some of the new college kids we acquired in June?"

"I remember Steve and Roger telling me the same exact thing the day you arrived."

I sighed heavily. "What now, Tom?" I aged ten years in two minutes as I gave into Tom's request.

"I told Sam that you'd be visiting him this week. He knows who you are and he'll discuss his projects with you. Why don't you pick a few of them that you think you can handle? Make sure you don't overextend your workload."

"I'm already trying to make room for the Management Development Program, Tom."

"I know, but this is the way it's going to be around here for a year or so."

I was at sea without a rudder. Wait till Lynn hears about this. "Tom, this won't work for me."

"I'm really sorry, Scott, but I've already tried to talk to Ira and he didn't want to hear about it."

I leaned against the wall, feeling bleak, depressed, and defeated. I had no more to give yet the company just kept demanding more. I wanted to quit right then. Tom walked over to me and rested a hand on my shoulder. "You can do it, Scott. Doug and Roger were annoyed, too."

"But they're not going to the MD Program."

"For your information, Scott, they didn't want to go."

That stunned me. Why wouldn't they didn't take advantage of the opportunity?

"Well, I need to finish these reports, Scott. Let me know by Monday at the latest which of the projects you decide to take over from Sam. One more thing. Get to know the old guy. You might learn a few things from him."

What in God's name could I learn from that old guy? Pension planning? Suddenly, an old pain entered my mind and now was the time to get it out. "Just one more thing, Tom."

"Yeah, what is it?" Tom was irritated. He'd thought we were through.

"Remember last week when you and Doug ripped me to shreads?"

He looked wary.

"What did you mean when you said, 'Go upstairs to Ed Vernan, the guy who hates the sight of you'?"

"Do you really want to know?"

"Let me have it."

Tom sighed. "You've never made a good impression on Mr. Vernan. Your name has been brought to his attention many times—and Ira's, too, for that matter—but for some reason, you don't get much respect."

"That's fucked-up, Tom! I've been busting my balls for those two!"

"Regardless, Scott. You're truly stuck between a rock and a hard place."

"And what's that?"

"It's not a textbook case, Scott. This is the real world, the school of hard knocks. Many people have gone through the same frustration and hardship as you have."

"Cut the bull, Tom. What are you saying?"

"Let me put it to you this way. You slave like a mule for the company. You work hard and all that good stuff, right? Most of your values are company-related and most of your life is focused on the company. It's obvious that you've given up your soul for the company."

I listened carefully to what Tom was saying. My inner voice spoke clearly: Is he being straight with me? Are his perceptions of me really true?

"The shitty part of it all, Scott, is that many senior executives like having guys like you working for them because they get the biggest bang for their buck. You give more and get paid less than almost anyone here. Unfortunately, senior people have no respect for someone who gives up his life for the company, someone who abandons his home and personal life. You're seen as a patsy, a loyal workhorse, a mule."

I went back to my office numb, with the words 'corporate mule' ringing in the recesses of my mind.

"On one hand, you're great to have around but on the other, you're never considered to be part of the corporate team. You'll end up treading water somewhere in middle management, coping and hoping that something other than retirement will come out of it all. Usually they plant you before they promote you."

A deep, dark anger rose up in me. All my dedication summed up to one thing: I was a corporate mule. I went back to my office numb and with the words "corporate mule" ringing in the recesses of my mind.

My black mood lingered through Thursday. Ben walked in unexpectedly. "You look down in the dumps today, kid."

"Naw! How can you tell?"

"What's wrong, Scott?" Ben was genuinely concerned.

"Just about everything imaginable. Life has been treating me kind of rotten lately and I'm finding myself more depressed each day."

"Life is neutral, Scott. It waits for your response before it hands you the next chapter. You're the one who's in charge. The responsibility for your thoughts and actions is on your shoulders."

"Oh, Ben, everyone's trying to tell me something. I'm tired of it all. I need at least a two-month vacation from this place— and from my wife."

"Your wife?"

"She's always on my case for working as hard as I do at this place. When I tell her that I want to become a vice president, she just screams in my face."

"Why is that, Scott?"

"She doesn't think I have the brains or skills to make it big. I'm sick and tired of trying to prove her wrong."

"Sounds to me, Scott, like Lynn loves you very much."

"I feel inferior next to her, or she makes me feel inferior. What's the difference? What's the use?"

"Do you ever stop to listen to yourself, Scott?"

"All too often. I get scared at some of the things I hear myself say. As a matter of fact, I've been dreaming about CSC more than I'd like to. It's beginning to drive me nuts."

Ben brightened. Here was something for him to explore. "What are you dreaming about? Work? Finishing projects? Getting the job done and pleasing Ira and Mr. Vernan?"

I didn't answer. What was the point?

"Boy, Scott. It sounds as if you really do need a long vacation. Is there anything I can do to help you?"

"Not that I know of, Ben." I thought for a moment. "There is one thing I'd like to ask."

"What's that?"

"Why are you so patient with me? I mean, you seem to truly take an interest in me. Why?"

"Good question, Scott. It's my nature and personality, I guess. Anyway, there are a few things I wanted to share about me. First, I was recently appointed by Fretman as the director of the Management Development Program, something that I've wanted for a long time. A memo should be out on Monday. Second, it's my sincere intention to get hard-working guys like you the recognition and visibility you deserve. That's a selfish goal on my part."

The locomotive at the end of the tunnel went into reverse and let the light shine in. At last there was someone on the planet whom I could trust and call a friend. A big smile lit my face.

"That's great, Ben!" My face hurt from the width of my grin. It was a rare expression for me.

After a brief and warm exchange, Ben went on. "Suppose you owned your own company."

"Yeah?" I wondered where he was leading me.

"Wouldn't you agree that if all of your employees performed their best, that the company would also function better?"

"I guess so."

"What would you do to encourage your workers to do their best?"

"Pay them more money?"

"Nope! That won't do it."

"I'd motivate them," I offered in earnest.

"How?"

I really was stuck this time. "I don't know, Ben. I really don't know."

"Well, wouldn't you want them to feel good about themselves? Develop themselves and be recognized for it, too?"

"Yes, I would. Yes."

"That's what's missing here at CSC. People like you burn out, lose your self-esteem and confidence, then give up and leave. The company has to constantly start all over again training someone new who will also only last a few years."

Yes. Ben's right. I felt supported somehow, less alone.

"Needless to say," Ben continued, "you lose your self-image. Your attitude turns sour so you look back bitterly instead of forward eagerly. Then you take your depression home with you where you get bombarded some more. Right?"

"Right you are."

I thought of Lynn's constant nagging as a thorn in my side. If I told her something great about CSC, she'd challenge me. If I told her something bad about CSC, she'd heartily agree and add something of her own. Walking into my house was like picking my way through a minefield.

I suddenly realized that I was sinking in a lose-lose situation at home, with no way out.

Chapter 13

TAKE A CHANCE!

For the next three months, I packed in sixty-hour weeks and still fell behind on my projects. The MDP class sessions varied. They were either very interesting or just plain boring. My commitment to pick up Richard at the nursery was broken almost immediately, except for Fridays.

Richard and Lynn slipped further down on my list of priorities. Actually, my relationship with Lynn had become quite cold. Our sex life was almost nonexistent. Backing off from Lynn at night because I wasn't in the mood made her furious. I couldn't get Ginger off my mind, and that didn't help. Since Richard needed more attention, I spent most of my time at home with him. This also gave me some relief from Lynn's constant attacks on me.

The week before Thanksgiving found me and most of my MDP classmates already despondent. We had six more months to slog through before we graduated and it seemed even longer when we thought about it.

The detailed courses in cost accounting and financial reporting were hard for me to grasp. The less painful topics dealt with management philosophy and its application in the work setting. The most challenging class focused on small group speaking skills.

I arrived at class early on Wednesday, the day before Thanksgiving. Training Room B was filled with four large work tables placed so that everyone could see everyone else during discussions. Video cameras and monitors were placed strategically around the room. The participants were from different departments throughout the company and each of us had assigned seats. Mine was in the front and on the right. Prior to the course, I'd made a personal request to Ben for that privilege because it had been my lucky seat in college.

As I looked around the empty room, I was saddened by an event that had happened there the day before. Nick Giamonte, a fun-loving artist from the Advertising Department, claimed that he was under too much stress and gave thirty days notice. One hour after submitting his resignation, he was told to pack his bags and leave. I can only imagine how bad he must have felt.

My mood passed and I began looking forward to that day's class. Ben was starting a month-long unit on Effective Presentation Skills. I felt honored to be in Ben's class.

As the other participants drifted into the room, they began chit-chatting with each other. The two women in the class were getting all the attention they could stand from the guys clustered around them. It was just past starting time when Ben walked briskly into the room with an apologetic smile. "You know," he said good-naturedly, "it's not smart to come to your first training session late — especially in this place."

The class chuckled nervously. After all, Ben was management to them and they weren't ready to let their guard down just yet. The other instructors were formal and business-like, but Ben was different. A new sense of interest began to pervade the room.

"Okay, y'all!" Ben said, "we've got a lot of ground to cover and a lot of surprises to exchange."

"Surprises?" one of the students asked. "What kind of surprises?"

"For one, we're going on a field trip to Disney World."

The class responded with laugher. "Yeah, right!" a guy with thick glasses said. "And this isn't CSC, it's Looney Tunes!"

"And then we'll have a party Friday night. I'll buy the beer and wine; you all bring the food," Ben said, his eyes twinkling.

Talk about surprises! What an unusual suggestion from someone in our very conservative company.

"Well, all right, now," Ben cheerfully went on. "We've got another surprise for you that will definitely get you on you feet. As you know, this course is titled, *Effective Presentation Skills*. After careful consideration, I have renamed it, *Presenting Your Self-image*. Isn't that great?"

Silence. Then Ellen from the legal department giggled and said, "Excuse me, Mr. Roberts, but is that the big surprise?"

Ben radiated confidence. His enthusiastic "Yes!" complemented his nonverbal body language. He was in control and I sat back to enjoy his style as he continued to address the group.

"A vital part of this training will, by its nature, focus on you as an individual. You will all have the opportunity to learn a lot more about yourselves. You will also share some of your discoveries about yourself with other members of this great group."

Ellen raised her hand again. "Mr. Roberts?"

"Please, call me Ben."

"Okay, Ben. What's so special about changing the name of the course?"

"I've changed more than the name," Ben said. "I've also changed the content of the course and brought in video cameras. We'll use them extensively to give each of you feedback on the way you present yourselves."

Ben continued his orientation. He walked towards me and rested his hands firmly on my table. Leaning toward me he said, "In this class we are going to talk about you. We are going to talk about your values, your ability to present yourself, your ability to properly confront yourself and confront difficult people. But most importantly, we'll talk about your ability to perceive your environment, especially the audience that you'll find yourself in front of."

Sensing something coming, I looked at Ben and asked, "What audience?"

The entire room was silent, waiting. Ben pulled back from me, turned toward the group, and answered in that wonderful way of his. "The most important audience you'll ever face is yourself. You must bear witness to who you are and what you do all the time. You must confront yourself and recognize the good you have done and reward yourself for it. You must also recognize when you come up short and rectify it."

The participants became more attentive. Something different was happening. Ben continued. "The second most important audience you'll ever face is your spouse. He or she serves as your witness for what you say and how you act.

"Your third most important audience will be management, especially corporate management. Do you know that Ed Vernan, your executive vice president, can *make* or *break* you in seconds? I've watched young folks like you fall apart in front of this man and flush their entire career with this company down the drain."

I was mortified at Ben's words, as though he was talking about me to the whole class. My face turned red and I wanted to crawl under the table and hide.

"I guarantee that if you do well in the Management Development Program," Ben said, walking around the room, "you will have a higher probability of success in whatever job or career you're in. But for now, you will find out much more about yourself than you think you know, some of which might be a shocking surprise to you.

"We've got twenty-two weeks ahead of us, folks. For this topic, we will meet twice a week. If you need to discuss anything personal with me, please feel free to do so. I commit myself to offering any assistance you may need and I will do the best I possibly can to help. But you must ask."

The Thanksgiving turkey was smaller than usual. I loved bread stuffing, but this time Lynn had chosen to try something different. My mother used to do the same thing. She'd get something down pat, then change it. Now I had to eat a horrible rice and sausage stuffing.

"Richard, bless his heart, loves the stuffing, don't you, sweetie?" Lynn said, patting his head.

When she went to the kitchen to get more dinner rolls, I spooned my portion onto his plate. By the time Lynn returned, Richard had eaten half of it.

Lynn was quiet throughout most of the meal. Richard received the majority of the attention and he loved every minute of it. If Lynn could be as patient with me as she was with her son, I'd feel a lot better. Needless to say, she was still harping at me for staying at CSC.

"The mashed potatoes are great, Lynn. You make them better than my mom."

Lynn looked at me with suspicion. "Were her mashed potatoes lumpy or something?"

"No, not really."

"Then what was it, Scott?"

"Ah ... just different."

"Come on, Scott. Say it!"

"Say what?"

"Say why you don't like the way I make my mashed potatoes!"

"But I do!"

"Bullshit! You don't have the balls to admit what's on your mind."

"Damn it, Lynn! There you go again. Shooting off your big fat mouth! Why are you always on my case?"

"I've had enough of your childish crap, Mr. Hendrick!"

Lost for words, I immediately stuffed more turkey into my mouth and almost choked. Lynn looked as though she wanted to cry. Then Richard began to scream in fear and protest. With my mouth full, I gestured to Lynn to go to Richard's rescue. I could have just as easily consoled him, but I played the macho, calling the shots.

Lynn looked at me in disgust. She pushed back her chair and vented her anger and frustration. "Shit! Shit! Shit!" She grabbed Richard protectively and ran out of the room.

I gulped down some water and sat there alone for five minutes, playing with my mashed potatoes. The grease in the turkey pan had begun to congeal into blobs of white fat. Lynn and Richard never returned to the table.

I turned on the TV to watch the New York Giant's football game. It was raining in New York, my hometown. The field was so muddy it looked like both teams wore the same uniform. New York. Suddenly I was assailed with homesickness.

I dialed my mom and dad but hung up before they could answer. Then I thought, what the hell and dialed again. Mother answered.

"Hello?"

"Hi, mom. Happy Thanksgiving."

"Scott! How come you haven't called for so long?"

"The phone works both ways, mom."

"True. How's Lynn and little Richard?"

"They're fine, mom."

"Did you call about anything in particular? We were just leaving to go to dinner."

"You're not cooking on Thanksgiving?"

"No. My arthritis is too bad this time of year. Do you want to talk to your father?"

"I suppose I could say hello."

There was a clatter she put the phone down. It was a good three minutes before my father answered. "Yeah?"

"Happy Thanksgiving, dad."

"Same. How's the job, boy? You make vice president yet?"

"No yet."

"Well, what are you waiting for? I thought for sure you'd be there by now. It's been a lot of years. What did we send you to school for? Aren't you going to make us proud?"

"Yeah, dad. It's just that with the stock falling and all that, there's been some belt-tightening. Cutbacks. You know how it is." My stomach flipped and tightened into knot, and I felt like I was about to lose my dinner.

"Well, let us know when the big day happens. I gotta go. Mother's already in the car. I'm taking her out for dinner."

We didn't even bother to say good-bye. I hung up the phone and reached for the bottle of Tums. My hand shook as I popped the cap.

Lynn was still in Richard's bedroom, with the door closed. The house was empty and cold. So was my heart. Then I heard Ginger's sweet voice in my mind. I thought of calling her but decided it would be dangerous to call from here. Fuck it. Anger overcame caution. I dialed her number.

"Hello, Ginger?"

"Scotty! I was hoping you'd call."

"How was your day? I hope it was better than mine."

"Oh, Scotty. I wish we could spend the holiday together. I miss you so much."

"Yeah, me too."

"Tell me what happened, Scotty. Talking makes it better."

She was so receptive and calmed me down with words that warmed my heart.

During the holiday season, time seemed to contract. There were too many things to do and, of course, not enough time to do them. Between my regular projects, Sam's old projects, and the MD Program, I became even more fragmented within myself. Tom McClane began to post late warnings on my computer's e-mail.

I had to cancel two trips to the regional office. The Program's reading assignments had to be done at home and that aggravated Lynn further.

I enjoyed Ben's sessions above all the others. The classes made me think. An important element surfaced in the program that I discovered was absent from my life: trust.

"Come on, Scott!" Ben shouted from behind the camera. "Trust me. Try your presentation again from the beginning."

"But I can't seem to get it right, Ben," I protested weakly. I had just died in front of the camera and my classmates, jumbling words and tripping up on my tongue.

"Say it!" he demanded.

"Damn it, Ben! I can't."

"Now, Scott!" he persisted.

"How about tomorrow?"

"Trust me, Scott. You can do it! Just trust me."

I looked around and saw all my classmates rooting for me. I was surprised to see such camaraderie expressed toward me. I gave it one last try. Facing the camera once again, I repeated

my lines. With the help of everyone's enthusiasm, I found myself sailing right through the presentation.

The group broke into applause. Ben was jubilant. "That's
great!"

Some of the guys whistled; the gals cheered. I couldn't recall having had a sensation like this in a long time.

After class, I met with Ben and he offered to buy me coffee.
As we walked to the snack room, he said, "You know, Scott, for
a minute I thought you were going to quit on me. But you came
through, as I knew you would."

I was still high from the session and I kind of blanked out
mentally.

"Did you see your face on the video replay when you said
'Damn it!'?" he asked, handing me a cup of coffee.

"Yeah. I was so frustrated! But something special happened
to me the moment after."

"What was that?" Ben asked, taking a chair and pulling it
out to sit down.

"I trusted you." My mind echoed the words, "trusted you."
It was a new experience for me. Somehow, the anger that had
welled up in me carried me beyond the fear that had become
my constant companion. Something about Ben had allowed
me to open up and see a part of me I didn't know was there.

Ben smiled and relaxed. "Thanks, Scott. I've been waiting
for this moment for a long time."

"Ever since I left New York, I've been alone. You're the only
person I've ever trusted."

"Why is that?"

"'Cause no one truly cares about me."

"That's not true, Scott. How about your wife? Me? Your
little boy definitely cares about you."

"Well, certainly Richard does, but lately my wife has given
up on me."

"Don't you believe that your wife cares for you and wishes
you the best?"

"Not really. I mean, I believe she cares for me as long as she
can get something out of it."

"Wait a minute, my friend. If you believe that, then you're living one hell of a lonely life. When I was behind the camera taking pictures of you, Scott, I was rooting for your success one hundred percent. There was nothing in it for me other than the joy of watching you grow."

Affected by Ben's sincerity, I began to realize the power contained in trust and devotion. He trusted his own convictions. I didn't even know what mine were.

After a few sips of coffee and some pretzels, Ben began a conversation that dramatically altered my life. "Scott," he said, "what do you think of me and my role at CSC?"

I gulped. "Well, Ben, you're definitely headed for the top!"

"Oh?" Ben reacted with surprise. "Is that so?"

"Uh-huh. You're probably one of the few people I know who understands his place in this organization. You have a great position, contribute directly to the company, and know more about what and where the company is going."

"Really, now!" There was a hint of mock amazement in Ben's voice.

I had a feeling that Ben wasn't buying what I said. "Isn't that true?" I asked.

"It's somewhat exaggerated, Scott. There's something I must tell you. But, please, it must be kept in strictest confidence. I'm only going to tell you now because you may truly learn from it. Do I have your word that you won't repeat any of it to anyone?"

I was confused, but vowed my secrecy in order to hear what Ben was holding back.

"How well do you know my boss, Grant Fretman?"

"Not very, except for a few superficial interactions here and there."

"Well, here's the inside scoop. Three weeks after appointing me as director of the MD Program in August, Grant and I had an unpleasant conversation. He told me to come down hard on a few of you in the class. Naturally, I inquired why. He told me that both Ira and Ed had suggested to him that I ax a few of the low performers from this class. By doing so, corporate management could send a message throughout the company that CSC would not tolerate mediocre performance. I didn't agree with that philosophy one bit. My position is firm: I feel individuals who are mediocre shouldn't be selected to attend the program in the first place. Instead, management should identify low performers early and try to help them. Well, the discussion went on until I asked Grant the critical question."

"Which was?"

"If he had challenged Ira and Ed's suggestion. He said he wouldn't think of disagreeing with either of them. Because I remained firmly opposed to sacrificing a few low performers, Grant and I were deadlocked. We resolved it my Grant agreeing to convey my feelings to Ira and Vernan.

"A week after the program began, Vernan called me in. When I reached his office, Ira and Grant were present. The place felt like a death trap. Vernan asked me to sit down. Then Grant said, 'I've repeatedly told you, Ben, that you must recommend at least two people to be dropped from the class. He went on, beyond what he had previously told me, and said I should also drop anyone who has a poor attitude about the company.

"I I reminded Grant that when I opposed the suggestion to drop two poor performers, he agreed to go back to Ira to further discuss my opposition to their suggestion. Now Grant was falsely claiming that I had agreed to terminate at least two people."

"That sucks, Ben," I said. I never thought that men in corporate positions would be so manipulative, but I believed Ben.

"You haven't heard the best yet, Scott." Ben propped his elbows on the table and rested his chin on folded hands. "Then Ira grunted and turned toward Grant as if to say, get on with it, boy! Grant, who looked sheepish, tried to cover his ass with more bullshit. Grant said to me, 'You're just not cooperating with us, Ben. First you say you will, and then you come here and deny everything we agreed upon. I'm very displeased with your performance.' "

I couldn't believe what I was learning from Ben. It all sounded so childish to me. Grown men didn't act like that, did they? Ben cut into my thoughts.

"To sum it up, Scott, Ira then turned to Ed and they nodded to each other. Vernan said, 'Ben, we've really appreciated your work at CSC, but this kind of behavior is not acceptable.'

"I looked at the three of them sitting in the Men's Hut and realized that they had already made a decision as to my fate with the company. My personality, my values, and my vision for a better corporation were not acceptable to them."

"I think that if I were in your shoes, Ben, I would have collapsed right then and there."

"Well, Scott, I took a chance, despite their warning. I rose up from my chair and said, 'Gentlemen, your point is clear, but your attempt to distort the truth is obvious and shameful. My loyalty to CSC is steadfast but I can no longer serve you unless you apologize. My integrity demands that I confront those who are morally impaired, who hide behind lies, and who lack the decency and respect for others.' They were stunned. Then I told them, 'I have nothing else to say,' and literally walked out."

"It's a wonder, Ben, that you're still around. It's amazing how well you stood up to them. But what were the aftershocks?"

"I'm still here, Scott, but the clock is ticking. I know that they need my services. I have an excellent track record and I'm not afraid to confront an adversary. But I do know that their egos have been challenged and that they are the ones in power. If I'm to survive and get a paycheck in this lifeless place, but lose my integrity in the process, then the price is too high."

I went for refills of our coffee and when I returned, I tried to get a few things straightened out in my mind. "How on earth can all this be true? Hasn't Fretman gotten back to you since then?"

"Not once. They're probably trying to recruit a replacement for me, but can't find someone cheap enough with my credentials."

"You're loved and liked by most of the people I know. And look where you are in the company."

"Thanks, Scott, but being a lovable guy doesn't mean you're going to get to the top."

"You're also a great instructor and motivator. All the guys in the class feel that you're the best instructor in the company and that you always put their well-being first."

"I take pride in my work because I'm a professional. That's why you all support me. The truth all boils down to one thing, Scott: know yourself. As far as where I am in the company, it doesn't mean much if no one is backing me. No matter how well you do, the higher up you go, the greater the challenge. And the greater the challenge, the more you have to be all you are and the best you can be."

We walked out of the snack room. I stopped at my office to get a few things and proceeded to the elevator. With my mind reeling from Ben's story, I heard nothing of what went on around me. As I waited for the elevator, I noticed Maria munching away on cookies while talking on the phone. I chuckled and thought of how lucky she was to live in total oblivion.

The elevator door opened. It was empty and I slowly walked in. During the ride down, I reflected on what I had learned today. Ben was in a serious situation. He had taken a chance and confronted his superiors. He may have lost his job, but he hadn't lost his integrity.

When the elevator door opened to the lobby, I felt a surge of energy rush through me. Ben's situation gave me a new perspective on life. Dealing with issues as they arose was something I was never taught before.

Then I heard my inner voice say, "Let go and be."

Chapter 14

IT'S TOO LATE!

With Christmas only two weeks away, the MD Program was on hold for the holidays. That was a great relief for everybody. I had a chance to catch up on work projects and cut back on my hectic work week. It was also a time to catch up on the latest company politics.

Doug walked into my office late one morning, very annoyed, and said, "Damn, it's hot outside."

"In New York," I offered, "the winters can be brutal and there's always a good chance for a white Christmas. But in Atlanta, what can you expect?"

Doug began to laugh, "You know, Scott, we had our worst snow storm here in eighty-two. Without warning, we had four inches of snow and the city came to a complete halt. The whole city shut down for two days. Can you imagine that?"

"Four inches of snow? What's the big deal?"

"Atlanta hadn't had snow for forty-two years. People even made T-shirts about it."

I personally thought the warm weather was a treat. On the other hand, I missed having a white Christmas.

"Anyway," Doug said, "since you're out of class, how about you and I going for lunch at the deli-cafe in the mall?"

"Sounds good to me."

We walked out into the sunshine. The temperature was a pleasant sixty-nine degrees. Many of the trees still held their autumn colors and it was a peaceful stroll. Doug seemed to have mellowed a bit. He was quite cheerful and vibrant for a family man in his mid-forties.

My stomach was growling. Even flirting was less important than my need for food. Doug kept stopping to window shop. I grew restless.

"Come on, Doug. Can't you hurry it up?"

He turned around and asked, "What's your problem, boy?"

"I'm hungry. Come on," I begged.

Doug got instantly hostile. "Suck on your thumb!" he lashed out.

"What do you mean, suck my thumb?"

"You're a corporate ass, Scott."

"Corporate ass?" I was bewildered.

"You bet."

"Here we are, enjoying our walk together, and all of a sudden you're coming down on me. You're a pompous jackass." I decided to back off and let Doug do his thing. We eventually found the deli-cafe.

"What'cha gonna have, boys?" the pretty deli clerk cooed.

"Give me a bologna on white with a little mustard to go," I answered.

Doug was interested in more than a sandwich. Looking at her name tag, he said warmly, "Billie-Jo. That's a real Southern name."

She gave him a real Southern smile, too. Why couldn't I have been that creative?

Doug leaned forward on the counter top. "Let's see, Billie-Jo. I'll have the same as my friend, Scotty here, but throw in a slice of Swiss and some lettuce."

"Coming up," said Billie-Jo.

"Say, Billie-Jo," Doug went on, "make Scotty's sandwich the same as mine. He could use a little cheese to liven up his bologna."

I was irritated by the put-down. Billie-Jo and Doug continued to flirt and eye each other's physical attributes. I became furious and interrupted the countertop duet. "No Swiss cheese for me, Miss Billy-girl."

She stared at me in disgust. "It's too late, sonny boy. The order is already in the computer."

"God damn it," I protested, "I hate Swiss cheese! Fix it the way I want it!"

Billie-Jo was taken aback and said, "Yes, sir. I'll fix it proper." Obviously disheartened, she began to assemble our sandwiches.

Onlookers in line behind us were very interested in the exchange. Doug turned to me.

"You've hurt the girl's feelings."

My face burned as Doug said, "Instead of responding with a positive suggestion like, 'Billie-Jo, I'll love you a lot more if you leave out the cheese,' you always manage to turn people away."

People in line nodded in agreement and I turned away in embarrassment. I saw the truth in Doug's reprimand and just wanted to hide.

Sam Hawkins from the programming division called and asked to see me. We agreed to meet before five for a brief planning session. Tom was depending on me to take over several projects from Sam, but I had pushed them to the bottom of my priority list.

I reached Sam's office by four-thirty. Because Sam was well respected by senior management, he had a cozy window office on the seventh floor, next to the library.

The wise-looking man greeted me pleasantly. "Come in, Scott, and have a seat."

"Hi, Sam." He should retire, I thought. Everything he does takes three times as long as anyone else. This was the third time we'd met in four months and he still hadn't gotten any project information or goals worked up. I wondered if Sam would be able to hand over the projects to me before he retired.

"Well," Sam said, "I guess it's about time you and I got to know each other."

I nodded my head. The truth of the matter was that I didn't care to, nor did I want to, waste my time getting to know this old dude. What the heck, he was going to retire. By the looks of the guy, he'd be more interested in pension planning rather than programming, anyway.

"Sam, I need to be out of here by five, if that's okay with you."

"What's the rush?" he asked calmly.

What's the rush? If this old geezer knew how much work I had to do, he'd say what he had to say and be done with it. Instead, we silently looked at each other for a couple of moments. Then he pulled out his pipe and fiddled with it. I don't need this, I thought, wearily. I don't need his projects. I don't need these headaches.

"Well," Sam said again, "what's the rush?"

I took a deep breath. As I readied to clobber him verbally, he said, "Damn it, Scott. Don't just sit there like a dumb old mule. Say something!"

I froze. My thoughts raced back into my past, triggering something inside of me. I had experienced this feeling before and I didn't like it. Why do people keep talking about damned mules?

Sam got up and moved toward the window. It was then that I saw his character for the first time. He was a diplomat, and looked like a wise, old sage. Looking down at me, he said quietly, "Listen, sonny, I've got other things to do. Now are you going to say something or not?"

Though he spoke quietly, I realized there was more to him than either his words or outward appearance indicated. "Yes, sir."

"Good. Tomorrow, you and I are going to spend the entire morning together, planning and discussing each project you've agreed to take on, so bring your note pad. Now you can leave."

I stood up next to Sam and realized that he was only about an inch shorter than myself. With his pipe in mouth, he puffed smoke in my face and I caught the aroma of his damn brandied tobacco.

He sensed my displeasure. "Don't worry, kid. You'll get used to me."

On my way home that evening, I couldn't get Sam Hawkins off my mind. Why did I freeze in front of him? He must have thought I was a jerk. And why did he get to me so easily? After all, he was retiring and was only a senior programmer. Why did what he thought about me matter anyway? I arrived home before Lynn and Richard. That was a strange sensation for me because I rarely arrived home before Lynn. The house was empty. There was no noise, no movement, no smell of food cooking, and no one to talk to. It was creepy. I didn't like it one bit.

I walked through each room, even into the large walk-in closets. Everything was as it should be. Maybe Lynn was playing a game with me. I meandered through the garage and then the back yard. Still no sign of the family.

Back inside, still wearing my suit jacket, I grabbed a cold beer and sat down in front of the TV. The usual stale reports about crime, tragedy, and disasters dominated the evening news. I changed channels but couldn't find anything that wasn't more of the same. Bored, I went to the kitchen in search of a snack and found an unopened family-sized bag of potato chips. I grabbed another beer and returned to the TV.

While stuffing myself with carbos, sodium, and fat, I watched a *Dynasty* rerun. During several childish commercials, I waited patiently, polishing off the bag of chips. Immediately following the commercials, the program credits rolled. I yelled at the TV, "What, the show is over? You tricked me into listening to those stupid commercials thinking the program would continue!" Angrily, I threw the empty beer can at the TV set.

With my mouth coated with grease, smelling of beer, and with an ailing stomach, I went upstairs and stretched out on the bed. In a few seconds I dozed off.

Sometime later, I was awakened by Richard's voice calling, "Daddy! Daddy!" Bewildered, I turned over as he reached the top of the stairs and ran to greet me. I hugged him and looked up to see Lynn smiling at the unaccustomed scene. She approached me and leaned forward to tap a kiss on my cheek.

"You've been drinking?" she asked.

"Just a couple of beers."

Sounding like my mother, Lynn said, "Mmmm." She walked into the closet to change while Richard began bouncing on my stomach. Though my head was dizzy from the beers and the day's work, Richard and I laughed and played. Lynn came out of the closet in just her panties as Richard dug his heel into my beer-laden bladder. His tiny butt came crashing down on my rebellious stomach. I was instantly sick and my head began to pound. I moaned and grinned weakly at Lynn. She came to my rescue and took Richard to his room to play.

The next thing I knew, Lynn slid her panties off and crawled on to the bed next to me with that old look on her face that meant only one thing. I suddenly had an urgent need to rush to the john. With pain in my bladder, potato-brew in my gut, and kangaroos in my head, I jumped off the bed, leaving my beautiful, naked wife lying there alone.

After relieving myself, I returned to be with Lynn, but she wasn't there. Feeling lousy about the situation, I got Richard and went downstairs to give Lynn a hug. I found her in the back yard. I put Richard down and walked up behind her. She stiffened when I put my arm around her.

"Stop that," she said, turning her back to me. The chill in her voice was menacing.

"There's another woman, isn't there," she said coldly.

Guilt washed over me. How did she know about Ginger?

"Well, is there?" she asked, beginning to cry.

I didn't know what to say. My head was pounding and I felt like I was about to throw up. The faces of Lynn, Ginger, Richard, and a host of folks from CSC swirled in my head. I just stared at Lynn, dumbfounded.

Lynn took my silence for guilt, and I could see the mixture of hurt, grief, and anger on her face as tears filled her eyes.

As I stood up, she struck me weakly in the chest and, sobbing deeply, went back into the house. She walked like someone who had just collapsed totally under overwhelming defeat.

I followed her into the house.

"How dare you! Another woman!" The tears spilled down her face as she turned to face me in the kitchen. I stood there like an idiot, not knowing what to do or say. By not immediately denying that I hadn't been unfaithful, I'd blown it. Now Lynn would never believe me.

We spent the evening in separate rooms. Richard darted back and forth between us, getting all the attention he wanted, innocently preventing us from killing each other. I spent the night on the sofa.

The next morning, I heard Lynn cooking breakfast. The aroma of bacon and biscuits got me up and I went upstairs to wash. I wanted to make sure that I arrived at work early so I could prep for my visit with Sam Hawkins or else he'd really be on my case.

When I entered the kitchen, Richard was in his highchair, playing with his food. I knew I had to talk to Lynn, but I didn't know how to tell her that I wasn't having an affair, but I was just seeing another woman for companionship.

"Well, Scott," she said, getting right to the point, "what do you have to say about this other woman?"

I crumbled. How can I say anything without hurting her? It's not that serious? What's the big deal, anyway? I hesitated, then said, "I'm not having an affair. I'm just being friendly with this person."

Lynn set a plate of biscuits, bacon, and scrambled eggs in front of me. "Damn it, Lynn. I don't like my eggs cooked that way."

Richard stopped messing with his food and looked at both of us.

At first, Lynn didn't acknowledge my protest, but then she said evenly, "The change was good for my soul."

I wasn't in the mood for spiritual stuff. I just wanted to get to work and here she was, obstructing me. "You know exactly how to cook my eggs!" I yelled, dumping my confusion and frustration onto her.

She turned away from the toaster oven and walked to the other side of the table, next to Richard. "Day after day, month after month," she said in a controlled voice, "I've cooked for my dear husband. I even wash his clothes. I take his happy little son to the nursery and bring him home. I even go to work every day as a supervisor and deal with a hundred different people."

107

She moved closer to me. All I could do was stare. She crossed her arms over her chest and, in a low, steady tone, continued to mock me. "Hey, Mr. Selfish, how about *you* cooking a ham and cheese omelet for *me*? Cook your son some pancakes, too." Her voice took on a derisive tone. "And, my dear hubby, don't forget to pick up my skirt from the dry cleaner's on the way home from the nursery. Remember, sweetheart, to be home before six so that you can prepare supper for your lovely wife."

Her sarcasm goaded me to anger and I threw my napkin on the floor. "Shove it, Lynn! I'm going to work where I can get some peace and quiet. Who needs this shit?"

Lynn held onto her composure and said icily, "I certainly don't."

I was seething as the police officer ripped the speeding ticket from her book and handed it to me through the car window. Who the hell was she, anyway? Women shouldn't be cops!

Then she put her face near the open window and said, "The next time I see your car speed through a school zone, mister, it's going to be jail for you."

I got to the office parking lot at 8:45, which was unusually late for me. After searching all the aisles without finding a spot to park, I kept driving up the ramp until I reached the roof level. The lot was full so I had to drive an extra block to the company's auxiliary parking lot. Worse yet, it had begun to drizzle, fouling my mood even more.

As I entered my office, Tom McClane, newly promoted to Director of Data Processing, was sitting comfortably in my chair. "Hi, Scott. I've got exciting news for you," he said.

I was in a bad mood. Beyond caring anymore, I barely roused myself enough to grumble, "And what the hell is that?"

"Hold on, Scott. I don't need that kind of shit from you or anybody else." He got up and walked to the door of my office. "See me when you've cooled off."

If I'd had a gun at that moment, I would have used it. I was so low and depressed that all six and a half feet of me felt barely three inches tall. I plopped into my chair. On my desk was a 5x7 portrait of Lynn in her wedding gown. She was happily smiling in the picture but at that moment it felt like she was mocking me instead.

Sam was going to call soon regarding our meeting. Just then Ben walked into the office. What a relief. In his usual cheerful manner he said, "Good morning, Scott-eee."

The phone rang. "Hello, Sam ... Yeah ... I just got in and Ben Roberts just walked in ... That's fine ... nine-thirty it is ... 'bye."

"You're looking pretty bad there, Scott," Ben observed.

"Shit happens but for me, it comes in bushels."

"What's going on?" Ben asked

"Fights with the wife, speeding tickets, insubordination, the wrath of God—everything's on me today."

"The day's only beginning, Scott."

"Yeah, but I need to see Sam, then Tom. How about you and I going out for lunch?"

"Sure," Ben said. "We can talk a lot more away from this place, anyway."

"Thanks, Ben. That would be great."

Sam checked his watch the moment I walked into his office. I wouldn't dare be late and give Sam the opportunity to ridicule me.

"Sorry about the time, Sam."

"No problem. I used the extra time to write a note to my daughter," Hawkins replied calmly.

Taken aback by his abuse of company time, I snipped, "And you get paid for it, too!"

Sam grew stern. "Listen, kid, if you want to be a timekeeper, get a timekeeper's job. If you want to judge others, become a judge, but I don't need you coming in here and telling me how I should do my job."

"I'm sorry. I didn't mean it that way, Mr. Hawkins."

"It appears to me, Mr. Hendrick, that what you think and what you say have little in common." He raised his eyebrows to emphasize his words and watched to see how I would respond to his needling.

"Yes, sir."

"Sit down."

I sat in the chair, gripping the arms as if expecting a beating. Once again my mouth had led me into trouble.

"I've worked for this company since it began. My employee number is zero-zero-one-five. What's yours?"

"I think it's five-two-oh-six."

"There you go again. You *think* it's five-two-oh-six? The mind-mouth diffusion syndrome. Do you know that God intended the mind and mouth to work together?"

"Yes, Sam. What's your point?" I dug in and steeled myself for Sam's sermon.

"I've worked all my life, some forty-five years or so," he said. "I've seen many different companies, hundreds of bosses, and thousands of employees along the way. I've also met quite a few ego-baboons like yourself. You're the kind of guy who wants to become somebody. Since you cannot grow inwardly, you choose to make your job do it for you. Your fantasies are far beyond what your deeds demonstrate. Success, success, success! That's what your ambition is, isn't it?"

I was quite mortified as Sam waited for my response.

Finally, I mumbled, "Yes."

"One day you might realize, Scott, that success is in the process, the doing. It's the beauty and joy of getting there. What I know of you is quite the opposite. You're always complaining, seeking perfection, blaming others, and judging yourself as unsuccessful. Am I correct?"

Shocked by his knowledge and the accurate description of my troubles, I mumbled, "I'm afraid so, Sam."

"Look, Scott, I've been around so long I could write a book on the subject. Young guys like you come out of high school and college thinking they can conquer the world with one hand behind their back. Well, they soon find out they've been had. Young people like yourself are stubborn and over ambitious. You go for the gold and shut down any personal feelings that might get in the way of that. Right?"

"Yeah. I guess that's the story of my life," I said, hating his guts for seeing through me so clearly.

"Good."

"What?" I couldn't follow his thinking.

"It's good that you understand me, Scott," he said, with more warmth in his voice. "You've got to break some of your old work habits. Otherwise you're going to be in for a big nasty surprise."

"It's already too late."

"Well, you'd better think a lot harder about who and what you really are and where you're going, my friend."

Sam and I finally got down to working on the projects. He was sharp and knew a lot more about the technical aspects of his job than I'd imagined. We discussed the plans, goals, and specifics of each project. I was surprised to see how efficiently Sam went about his work. No wonder he had a lot of spare time.

On matters concerning myself, I took heed of what old Mr. Hawkins told me. He was honest, rather blunt, and to the point. I realized that, besides Ben, he was the only person who wanted to help me.

I stopped by Tom's office on the way back to mine. He'd left me a message to meet him after lunch.

Ben and I met at the Fortune Dragon Chinese Restaurant for lunch. He had a few free days because the MD Program was in recess. We had a cup of hot tea and the lunch special.

"So, what's all this stuff about the end of the world, the wrath of God, and the fights with the wife?" Ben inquired.

"I don't know what's been happening to me lately, Ben. Everything I do is wrong, especially when it comes to Lynn."

"You're saying a lot there, Scott. Let's focus for a minute on work. That usually seems to be the big one."

"I can't breathe anymore. No matter how hard I try to get ahead, something always sets me back. You know, the Eighty/

Twenty Rule: eighty percent of my activity results in twenty percent of my success."

"You're too hard on yourself and everyone around you, Scott. Worse yet, you always accept whatever anyone hands you without thinking. When was the last time you said no to anyone about work?"

"Last August, to Tom. He asked me to take over some projects from Sam Hawkins. But I had to do it."

"Ah, yes. Sam Hawkins."

"Do you know him?" I asked.

"Sure do. Sam and I go back a ways. He was one of the people who interviewed me for my job eight years ago. He's a very wise man."

"I spent some time with him this morning. I've grown to like him."

"He's one of the few people in this organization who can put it to you straight, Scott. He's a no-frills man."

"I'll say. He put it to me this morning. As a matter of fact, both you and Sam tell me the same thing."

"Yeah? Like what?"

"Like stop trying to be somebody else all the time. He even told me to say no, just as you did a few minutes ago."

"Is all this advice going to help you, Scott?"

"I hope so," I said, somewhat skeptical.

"You hope so? Listen, Scott, you have to get your mind and mouth working together. What your mind thinks and your mouth says don't always agree with each other. Hoping and doing are two different things."

I'd heard this no less than three hours ago. Someone was definitely sending me a message. "Then, how can I get my big mouth and dumb brain to work better together?"

"You'll need a mental enema. Try mixing together some Gator Aid and Drano. Pour it in through your ear, stand up-side-down, and shake yourself a little."

"Very funny."

"What you really need, Scott, is some free time, a little R and R, maybe some good reading. You also need to set realistic goals for yourself and your family."

"Don't mention my family."

"Why?"

"Lynn's always coming down on me. Every day there's something new and it's always my fault."

"How is she doing at work? Maybe she's having some problems of her own."

"I don't really know."

"What do you mean, you don't know?"

"Exactly that, Ben. I don't know how she's doing."

"Aren't you guys talking to each other?"

"Not really. Mostly we yell at each other. Last night I really fucked up. Lynn wanted to make love, but I felt sick and just couldn't. She started crying. Then she asked me about Ginger."

"Who's Ginger?"

"I don't feel like talking about this anymore."

"Scott, who's Ginger?"

"A woman I met at Richard's nursery. We usually go out for a couple of drinks together and stuff."

"Stuff?"

"No, not that kind of stuff."

"Not yet, anyway," Ben said.

"She's not married and likes my companionship, Ben, that's all."

"You're leading that poor girl on, Scott. She's probably waiting for you and Lynn to get a divorce."

"Come off it, Ben. Lynn's not going to leave me."

"I've got a feeling that you're in for more hard-core learning, Scott. It sounds all too familiar to me. You'd better get your act together with Lynn and this woman, Ginger, before all hell breaks loose."

After lunch, Ben went on an errand and I headed back to the office. There was another note from Tom in my e-mail. It said, "Unexpectedly had to go with Ira to Pittsburgh. Talk with you on Monday." That was fine with me. It gave me some unexpected spare time.

I spread out several project folders on my desk to review. With my shirtsleeves rolled up, I began a desperate attempt to catch up. Half an hour into my efforts, Maria strolled into my office.

"Hey, big guy, what's happening?" she asked in a lazy, suggestive voice.

"Nothing much. I'm busy right now." I was irritated at her for interrupting my concentration.

Maria decided to sit down. I didn't want her to do that. Not today, not ever.

"How come," she challenged, "you never talk to me or say hello anymore?"

"What do you want?" I asked. "Can't you see I'm busy?"

"You know, Scotty, my boy," she purred, "you think you're so special but you're not. You should know what *I* know about you."

What the hell is she talking about? "What do you know?"

"Well, darling, I work for Tom and Ira and I know just about everything that happens on this floor." She looked at me with a wouldn't-you-like-to-know expression.

I found myself not so much bothered by her company as curious about what she might have to say. "Well, then, Maria, how about sharing some of your corporate secrets?"

"Sure!" she grinned. "How about your projects being two months late?"

I grimaced and rolled my eyes. She read my body language well because her grin grew even wider.

"Want to hear more?"

Like a fool swimming with sharks, I nodded.

"Ira mentioned to me that you were buddying-up to Ben Roberts in order to get on Ben's good side."

"That's not true, Maria."

"Well, that's what Ira thinks. Want more, Scotty-boy?" She crossed her legs suggestively.

I really wanted her to go, but paranoia reigned. Maria was having a blast with me and I knew it. I should have insisted that she leave.

"Oh, I almost forgot to tell you, Mr. Hendrick," she said, leaning forward as she said my name, implying even more intimacy by moving closer to me, "Ginger-girl called this morning while you were with Sam Hawkins. She left a number to call her back."

Maria was obviously snooping regarding with my relationship with Ginger. If there was one person in this world I didn't trust, it was Maria.

"What did the lady want?"

"She was hoping you could meet her for lunch because she won't be able to see you tomorrow after work."

I'd had enough. I stood up and, with as much formality as I could muster, said, "Thanks, Maria. It's time for you to go. I need to get back to work."

Maria practically danced out of my office, happy that she had accomplished what she had set out to do.

I wondered if Ben and Sam were right. I was working as hard as I could and never got ahead. My dream of becoming a vice president was already three years behind schedule. Except for the project goals, I had not established any personal goals, much less family goals—not even a vacation.

Maria had truly upset me. Was it *what* she said or *why* she had said it? Did she really hate me? Did I hate her or was I just frustrated with myself?

"Hey, shithead!" Doug called from my doorway. "Are you all right?"

I knew he meant well. "Come in and sit down, Doug. I'm okay. What's up?"

He handed me a file. "I got this project from Sam Hawkins. After a careful review, I thought you would be the best person to handle it."

I looked through the folder and realized he was right. We discussed the project for an hour. Now I had even more work to do in my spare time. Once again, I hadn't had the courage to say no. Once more I had contributed to my own self-destruction.

Needing a break, I took a walk outside. Steve and Roger were sitting on the shady steps, drinking Coca-Cola. I joined them. "Hi, guys."

"Hey, big guy," Roger teased, "have a seat."

We got into an interesting conversation about places to hike and fish. It was thirty minutes before I remembered I had lots of work to do.

"Hey, Scott," Steve asked as I got up, "where ya' going?"

"Back to work."

Steve waved my comment aside. "Screw work. It's Christmas time. Get into the spirit."

That made sense, after everything I'd been hearing all day. I had enjoyed our conversation. It had been a long time since I had even thought about fishing or being out in Nature.

Later, as I slowly walked to my office, I had an urge to drop all my troubles and fly away. I had always admired the eagle and its utter freedom.

Still immersed in my reverie, I saw Maria walking toward me in the corridor. An unexpected peaceful mood came over me. I didn't feel any animosity toward her. Instead, as she came near me, I smiled and asked, "Do you have an extra cookie for me?"

Her dark eyes opened wide with surprise. "Sure."

We walked over to her desk, where the cookie jar sat in one corner.

I munched contentedly on a jumbo chocolate chip/hazelnut cookie as I walked down the corridor to my office. How's that for change? I thought. Then I realized that I still had not actually accomplished anything productive that day. Was I so preoccupied with my problems that they caused me to fall behind in my work?

After weighing my thoughts and savoring Maria's cookie, I resumed the attack on my work. In the next ninety minutes I accomplished a lot. It finally dawned on me that top performers who work with a positive attitude enjoy what they do. Sam and Ben were right: get your mind and mouth to work together if you want to see positive results. I felt great for the first time that day.

The phone rang twice. Two fast rings signaled an outside call having nothing to do with work.

"Hello, this is Scott Hendrick."

"Scott," Lynn said, "we need to talk about plans for the weekend."

"Sure," I said jovially. "What's up?"

"How about taking your son to the zoo?"

"If I have the time, sure!" My stubborn mind wanted to say no to Lynn but another part really wanted to be with my son.

"Make the time," Lynn said. "I need a break."

"Here we go with your damn complaints again."

"Your son needs you, Scott."

"Yeah, I know that," I sighed, softening just a little. "What does he want to do?"

"Why don't you ask him? You're his father."

"Okay."

There was a pause before Lynn continued. "Do you mind if we ask Jim and Angie over for a cookout?"

I thought this would be a good opportunity to crack a joke to get some life back into our conversation so I said, "I'd like to have you for dinner, sweetheart."

"What the hell do you mean with that stupid remark?"

"I was just teasing you, Lynn."

"I bet you really meant something by that."

"Maybe I did and maybe I didn't," I growled. "Anyway, go ahead and invite your friends."

"My friends? You introduced them to me!"

"Look, I've a lot of work to do over the weekend."

"I don't need this. I've got to go," Lynn said.

"Go where?"

She didn't answer.

"Go where?" I repeated, my voice gaining an angry edge.

Her voice cracked, as though she fought back tears. "Anywhere I can find some human warmth and kindness."

I wanted to come back with some words that would make her feel better, but the sight of the huge pile of project folders on my desk knotted my guts and paralyzed me. What could I say without inviting more hostility? Lynn solved my dilemma by hanging up on me.

Sitting back in my chair with the same shitty feeling as I'd had earlier that morning, I felt Lynn's frustration and withdrawal. My troubled mind meandered in many directions, none of them soothing.

Chapter 15

WHERE TO NOW?

New Year's Day came in like a lamb and Lynn went out with a roar. Despite my unsuccessful attempts to curb my invidious tongue, Lynn's tolerance evaporated. The most important thing Ben had kindled in me was trust. Unfortunately, that was the one thing Lynn had lost in me.

I guess Lynn figured that my devotion to the company was stronger than it was to my family and that she couldn't win me back. And added to my list of problems was a new one: impotence. My inability to make love with my own wife was the last straw and she spent many cold nights alone, which broke her heart. Our inability to communicate had become an insurmountable barrier and when she announced that she was leaving and taking Richard with her, I wasn't really surprised and offered no resistance.

She had rented a small two-bedroom apartment a block away from her job and had packed her things while I was at work. Lynn came back later that night to get the last of her things. She put them in her car and came back into the house, and stood, hands on her hips, facing me.

"There's a few things I've got to say to you, Scott, before I leave. You blew it big time. You had a wife who loved you and a son who adored you, and you didn't even notice. All you cared about was your stupid job with its dumb lapel pin and your stupid Men's Hut. And do you think they give a damn about you?

"People loved you, and you turned away to chase some dumb dream of becoming a vice president so you could win your father's approval. And why? What has he ever done for you except get on your case?

"You've fucked up your marriage and your life. Well, I'm getting out while I still have a chance to be happy! I hope your new girl friend has better luck with you, but I doubt it.

"And don't even think about getting back with me, because you're a lost cause, mister. Have a nice life!"

And with that, she swept out of the house and my life, slamming the front door behind her.

It was a lonely time for me with a big house, lots of cleaning waiting to be done, a dried out Christmas tree, and a month's worth of bills to pay. Nothing could soothe the loneliness. How could I get my family back together?

January 2nd found me right back at CSC. No sooner had I arrived than McClane called me into his office and apologized for not getting back to me before Christmas. Then he informed me Ira had requested that I take on a special co-venturing project with an outside consultant.

Initially, I was excited. Then common sense returned. "Tom, I can't take on another project. I'm already working over fifty hours a week, plus weekends."

"Yeah, Scott, I'm well aware of your work load. Ira and I have been doing a lot of talking about you and your career at CSC."

A wave of panic gripped me and I began to sweat. My wife's left, my son's gone, now my job was in jeopardy.

"Scott," Tom said, interrupting my fear, "are you listening?"

Paranoid now, I grabbed a breath of stale office air and asked, "What's wrong?"

Tom looked perplexed. "Nothing's wrong."

I was breathless, my pulse pounding in my temple.

"Listen, Scott, you've got a couple of trustworthy friends here. Without either knowing about the other, Hawkins and Roberts approached me separately on your behalf. I shared what they told me with Ira and now he finally understands your dilemma. He wants you to slow down a bit. That's why we're going to change a few projects for you."

Tom and I discussed the details. Basically, I was to let go of my Regional Training project and several other tedious assignments. The projects Sam gave me as well as Doug's last minute project were critically important. Tom felt I was best suited to accomplish those tasks. Everything was in order for me to continue in the Management Development Program, which would restart on Thursday. This meant I would have a realistic job with manageable work hours. I would even have weekends to myself.

With that news I began to calm down and even managed a weak smile. There were just too many things happening for me to cope with, but maybe now I could start acting like a human being rather than an administrative robot.

The rest of the day moved along easily. I had the rare experience of delegating work to Steve, Roger, Doug, and a couple of new recruits. At four o'clock, I called Ben to thank him for his support. He acknowledged my thanks and asked me to come to his office to see how he'd changed the interior. I volunteered to bring the coffee.

When I arrived, we exchanged upbeat, hearty good wishes for the New Year. Ben looked relaxed in the midst of his new decor.

"Hey, Ben, the changes are something else," I said, approving of what I saw. The walls sported a new coat of a soft blue paint. There were two large silver-framed photographs of the San Francisco skyline on one wall. A new silver and black lamp graced his desk. Gone were all the Indian artifacts.

"You really like them, Scott?"

"I sure do. What prompted the change?"

"I wanted to take my personal stuff home since I've completed remodeling my den and the library. The stuff I had in here before goes better at home. It feels more comfortable. As for the new colors, I suppose they're kind of basic. You know, conservative with a slight fling to it."

"You're not the conservative type, Ben."

"For a while I'm gonna be. I'm tired of rocking the boat around here. I need to know what works and doesn't work for me around here. Sometimes we have to tighten up, sometimes we have to let loose."

"Come again?"

"Did Tom inform you that I spoke to him and Ira?"

"Yes, he did."

"I debated that move for several weeks. Prior to the Christmas break, I saw how stressed out you were. Burned out, I should say."

"With hindsight," I nodded, "I'd say that's very accurate."

"How long did you think you would've lasted in that state, Scott?"

"A couple of months, maybe."

"Optimistic, to say the least. In reality, Tom and I felt that you were at wits' end and ready to explode. If the conscience of CSC didn't take heed of your dilemma, it would lose you and, dollar-wise, that's a classical mistake. So you were the exception. The decision to support you overrode the company's usual intolerance in this matter."

"I really was ready to explode. I'm still at wits' end regarding my marriage."

Ben was concerned. "Did something bad go down at home?"

"Lynn took her things and little Richie."

"I'm sorry to hear that, Scott."

"I'm lost without them, Ben. As much as we quarreled, I never imagined her leaving me."

Ben offered to speak to Lynn, but I declined. It was my duty to rectify my marital problems.

Ben changed the subject and focused attention on the positive changes related to work. "When Ira and I spoke, he also brought up the time I confronted him, Ed, and Grant. Remember my telling you about that?"

"Very much, Ben."

"Well, in order to score some positive strokes in your favor, I made a few concessions, some of which you can already see in this room."

some serious thinking back over our relationship. I thought about the early months and the nights of making love until dawn. Where did all that passion go? How could two people who couldn't keep their hands off each other end up screaming at each other? What had happened?

It was ironic and sad that I was now down to forty-hour weeks—the very thing Lynn wanted most—but she was not around to enjoy my free time.

Maybe it wasn't all Lynn's fault. Maybe I had been overly consumed with my career and not made enough time for my family.

Lynn had talked a lot about love, but what was love, anyway? To me it meant being a good provider, and that meant hard work, but the harder I worked to prove my love for Lynn, the more angry she got. How could I win? Maybe we should have talked about our definitions of love. To me it was a doing thing; to her it was a feeling thing.

Ginger suddenly popped into my thoughts. Richard had switched day care, so I no longer got to see Ginger, but I decided to go to Richard's old daycare the next day. Maybe I could catch Ginger there.

The following day, Doug and I walked through the mall at lunch hour. Suddenly, Doug poked my side with his elbow and said, "Wow! Would you look at that!" He directed my attention towards a most gorgeous woman. Her long, shapely legs ended in a dress so short it hardly covered her rear, and most of her breasts were visible thanks to the generous arm-holes.

It was Ginger and she was definitely on the prowl. Decked out in that dress, she left little room for fantasizing. She saw us staring at her and then waved to me. We headed toward each other.

"Scotty!" she said gaily, announcing a reunion.

"Hi, Ginger."

"Where have you been?" she asked, her sapphire eyes brilliant.

"Busy with work and training."

"I've tried to reach you at work several times, but you're never there. I left my number with your receptionist, but you never called. I thought you'd given up on me."

"Oh no, Ginger. It was just difficult to call from work, and impossible from home. I can't believe the coincidence. I was actually going to try and see you at the day care place tonight. There's a lot happened that I want to talk to you about."

Her smile convinced me that she still had feelings for me.

Doug poked me in my ribs. I introduced him to Ginger. He exchanged only a few words with Ginger before I intervened. I didn't want him moving in on her with his macho routines.

"How about dinner this Saturday?"

"I'd love to, Scott."

"Great! I'll call you tomorrow and we'll talk more then, okay?"

Smiling happily, she waved as she left. Doug followed her with his eyes until I punched him in the arm.

With a sense of awe, Doug stepped in front of me and grabbed my shoulders. He looked me in the eye and asked, "Where did you meet her?"

"It's a long story, Doug. I'll fill you in on it, but not now. I've got to get my head on straight with this woman. She's a bit too aggressive for me."

"*I'll* take her!"

"You're married, Doug."

"I'll get a divorce."

"Bullshit, you will."

We headed back to the office like two high school studs bragging about the good old days. It was good to know I still had it in me to attract a beautiful woman. Doug was kind of fun, too. He was more relaxed. Or was it me who was more relaxed?

I woke Saturday and my first thought was of Ginger and our date that night. I lay in bed fantasizing about making love with her, picturing the two of us in wild sexual abandon, and was delighted to find that impotence was no longer a problem for me. But how much to tell her about Lynn was a problem. I didn't want to get into details because it was all still too painful and it would ruin the mood. I decided to play it by ear and hope my runaway mouth would not get me into trouble.

The fantasies continued all day and during the drive to her place. It was a small house, but neat and beautifully tended. I rang the bell, wondering what wildly sexy outfit she'd be wearing. My jaw dropped; she was dressed as though she was going to church—high neckline, low hemline and loose fitting.

Her welcoming smile was warm, open, and radiant. We touched hands briefly, and she said, "I'll just be a moment."

She called good-bye to Christy and the baby-sitter and came out.

"Scott, if you wouldn't mind, I'd like to go somewhere quiet. Like Stella's, maybe."

"Fine with me," I said, marveling at how, with her choices of dress and restaurants, she had set the agenda for the evening.

I opened the passenger door and she slid smoothly into the car, taking the hand I offered her. What a difference from the last time we'd met.

At the restaurant, valet parking whisked the car away, a table was ready, and we ordered drinks. When they arrived, Ginger looked directly into my eyes for a few seconds.

"Well, Scott, I don't know where we're going with all of this, but let's drink to love and happiness."

"To love and happiness," I replied, holding her gaze.

We ordered our food and Ginger rested her chin on her hands, looked deep into my eyes, and said, "So tell me what's been going on."

Despite my intentions to be guarded, in the fifteen minutes it took for our food to arrive, I'd summarized my entire marriage with Lynn, holding nothing back. Ginger was magnificent. Her body language and eyes signaled understanding when I admitted what a jerk I'd been, and compassion when I described how Lynn had hurt me.

"Quite a story," she said, smiling as the waiter arrived. "And now what?"

"I don't know, Ginger. Maybe I need a little time to get sorted out. But I know one thing. I'm having dinner with a beautiful woman I care a lot about, so let's forget everything else and eat."

The rest of the evening flowed enjoyably and smoothly. We talked about where we grew up and went to school, the weather, the Olympics, and a host of other neutral topics.

Back at her house, I escorted her to the front door, told her what a wonderful evening I'd had, and hugged her. She stood on tiptoe and we kissed briefly.

On the drive home, I smiled. The evening of my fantasies had not materialized and I was glad. I had the feeling that something much more important had happened.

Things were actually starting to smooth out for me at work. I met all my due dates on each project and did extremely well in the MD Program. I even had time to play around with my computer. One day Steve turned me on to a computerized fishing game he had designed. Within a couple of days, I had become addicted to it.

June arrived and that meant graduation from the MD Program was only three weeks away. Except for occasional dates with Ginger, I concentrated most of my free time on finishing the practicum for the program and spending time with Richard.

The graduation ceremony reminded me of the first Employee Orientation meeting. Members of the Men's Hut were present and capitalized on the event. Each of their respective speeches offered the thrills of corporate nonsense. My dealings with Ben and Sam had prepared me for the onslaught. I wished Kama was there. She would have really put some pizzazz into it. As it was, cap and gown and all, the ceremony went smoothly.

Ben got a special commendation for the excellent outcome of the program. His determination to stick to his values paid off—not one class member was terminated. I was proud to know Ben had scored a victory based on his principles and I wondered if I would ever have the balls to do what he had done.

Chapter 16

PARDON ME

Regaining an enthusiasm for life, I found myself meeting all my deadlines but doing less and less at work. As a matter of fact, I began to find ways to avoid it. A classic example was the infamous and endless string of meetings. The more time I spent in meetings, the less productive I became, therefore the more people I needed to get the job done. Ironically, not only was this acceptable to management but encouraged as "team-building." I wish I had known that right out of college.

Reflecting on it all, I was beginning to learn how to survive in the system. Each company has its own system of politics. Survival depends on knowing that system and the players within it. Sam and Ben succeeded because they understood it. They were able to find their place of balance within it—something I had failed to do.

In my spare hours at CSC, I thought a lot about what I had seen there over the years. I made a list of survival tactics, and put them into a new computer graphics program I was playing with. The result looked like a poster. My favorite elements were visibility, conformity, agreeing with the boss, keeping busy, talking out loud, saying only what had already been proven, secretly re-inventing the wheel, writing reports, not being creative, drinking with the bosses, and back-stabbing others for gain. These were just a few of the dynamic tricks to learn in corporate college. I was beginning to realize that having free time at work is advantageous if you want to get to the top.

I finally understood that the decision makers and the labor-ers were worlds apart. There are millions of employees like me out there who believe that hard work, loyalty, and dedication can get you to the top. Then I realized that you don't necessarily need expertize to get to the top. It's all in the chemistry—who you know and being in the right place at the right time. Most skills are learned on the job anyway.

I wanted to know about the people in the organization and how they perceived the workplace. Listening to the managers, then listening to the employees and comparing their views of things, was a great learning opportunity for me. Many of the guys at the top were typically game-players, usually in some form of inconspicuous combat. Male or female, it didn't mat-ter; each was out for themselves.

Occasionally, a true corporate hero would surface and re-focus the purpose of their department, or even the corporation, but the usual "cover your ass" attitude prevailed. Employees, on the other hand, possessed more zeal, initiative, and ambi-tion than anyone realized, but that didn't help them attain ownership in the corporation or help its direction.

It was the employees who built the product and serviced the customer but once an employee entered middle manage-ment, his ass was on the line. In management, substantial energies were channeled into covering your ass and surviving challenges from your peers. Staying alive personally became more important than keeping the company alive. A good strat-egy was to surround yourself with loyal scapegoats and instill fear into their egotistical minds.

I was learning about corporate survival fast. There wasn't anything wrong in having a couple of beers at lunch, either. It was good for your image, reduced stress, and made you feel cheerful. Tom and I began to take a few lunch breaks together and he was an invaluable source of inside information on office politics and corporate gamesmanship. I even took Maria out for Mexican food a few times. After two margaritas she became dangerous, but it was fun.

Life at CSC began to make sense. I was more comfortable and in control. I put in an honest day's work and, at the end of the day, was able to go to my empty house and relax. It wasn't that CSC had changed, it was I who had changed.

Ginger and I had been seeing more and more of each other, often dating two or three nights a week—movies, bowling, dinner—and she, Christy, and I would go for long walks at the weekends. Christy was beginning to accept me as part of her life and liked to sit high on my shoulders as we walked. Richard and Christy got on well, too, and would spend hours playing together.

Ginger and I would end our dates with kisses that became more passionate each time, and although we both knew that sex between us was inevitable, we were taking it easy, neither wanting to go too fast.

On the Thursday before Memorial Day, I meandered up to Ben's office to see what his plans were for the weekend.

"Hey, Scott," Ben welcomed, "how the hell are ya?"

"Just fine. I came to find out what your plans are for the weekend."

"I'm going to visit Kama in San Francisco." he said jovially.

Though I was touched by his candor, I was a little possessive about Kama, maybe even a bit jealous that it was he who was going and not me. "Kama? Really?"

"Yeah, she's excited about my visit. We were just talking, no longer than an hour ago."

I was still taken aback but managed to ask, "So, how is she doing?"

"Couldn't be better. She got another promotion and recently bought a condo in the Marina District."

"It sounds like she's doing quite well for herself."

With a curious smile, Ben probed my thoughts. "Haven't you been staying in touch with her, Scott?"

"No, not really, but I should. Maybe I'll call her tomorrow morning."

"The minute I mentioned Kama, you got melancholy, Scott. Is there anything wrong?"

"Naw. She brings back a few memories, is all."

"You liked her, didn't you?"

"Yes, but I was too ignorant to know it back then."

"By the way, how are you doing with Lynn and the boy?"

"It's weird. It's real weird. I still love her a lot and now I can see all the mistakes I made, but she's given up on me. Every time I go to pick up Richard, I want to hug Lynn and stay. Unfortunately, she's as cold as ice to me."

"Do you guys fight anymore?"

"Not one bit. We're actually kind to each other. It doesn't matter, though. She won't come back and take a chance with me."

"Is there another guy, maybe?"

"Nope. She doesn't want another male influence around Richard. Ever since I cut back on my long hours, I've been a real father to him. Anyway, Lynn will start on her doctorate in Human Resources Development at Georgia State next month and has already asked me to spend more time with Richard. I truly don't believe she's going to have any time for a man."

"That's a shame, Scott. That lady is sharp, beautiful—and in such pain."

On that note, we both became depressed. Then Ben clasped his hands and said, "All right now, that's enough of that."

We each took a deep breath and smiled.

"Well, Ben, it looks like you're gonna have some fun this weekend. I'll stay home and watch the Braves play baseball. I might...hey, maybe I'll take Richard to the Sunday double-header."

"Now you've got it working, Scott."

"So say hi to Kama and please give her a big hug for me, okay?"

On the way down from the tenth floor, I decided to detour and see Sam.

"Ah! My friend, Scott," he said. "Come on in."

"How are you doing, Sam?"

"Just super, my boy. Super!"

Sam's build was amazing for a guy his age. He wasn't the typical hacker but someone who could model for a Chevas

Regal ad in *GQ* magazine. He could change your attitude in seconds and make you think even faster just by the finesse of his own thoughts.

"I'm glad you came by to visit. I've heard a lot of good news about you lately and wondered how you were getting along."

"Graduating from the Management Development Program was a great relief."

Sam corrected me quickly. "A great achievement, you mean."

"And," I added, "letting go of several projects gave me the room to see daylight."

"Gave you the room to take the time to think things out, huh?"

I smiled at that one. "Yeah, Sam. I sure did do a lot of thinking. Lots!"

He smiled back at me as he reached for his pipe. Two puffs later, he said, "So, how are we on the projects?"

"Actually, Sam, we're ahead of schedule. If you don't mind, maybe you can review them for me."

"Stick that idea up the can, boy. They're in your hands now. Who needs that shit, anyway? There are more important things to do."

"Like what?" I challenged.

"Play some golf. Figure out my pension and retirement funds. Say *ciao* to all my hard-working friends. Spend some special time with you."

I took that as an honor. My chest expanded. Sam made me feel good. "That's a good plan, Sam."

"Ready for this, son? You're in charge of my retirement ceremony and party."

"What?"

"Yep! I volunteered you."

I really didn't want this assignment, but neither did I want to hurt Sam's feelings.

"Do you know a guy named Vernan?" Sam asked.

"Of course," I replied.

"He unexpectedly came down for a visit. We talked and he encouraged me to proceed with a formal retirement ceremony. I didn't want to bother with such a ridiculous event but Vernan insisted. I agreed on one condition. Get it?"

"Yes, indeed, Sam. And just when I thought I had a little extra time."

He grinned and took a few puffs on his pipe. "Let me know when you want to start planning. I've got all the time in the world."

With one day left before the holiday, I asked Ginger to spend the weekend at my house and she agreed.

On Saturday, the baby-sitter came over for the morning to watch Christy and Richard while we played golf. Ginger fared well on the golf course. She was a great teacher and introduced me to a challenging, yet fun-loving sport. I especially enjoyed her standing behind me with her arms around me to teach me to swing. I could feel her thighs, her belly, and her breasts against me, and I knew she was enjoying the sensation because she pressed harder than was necessary. The sexual energy just continued to build as we walked the golf course. Suddenly I asked Ginger to what she thought love was.

"Well, Scott, to me love is letting things and people be what and who they are. You know the saying, 'If you love something, let it go. If it loves you, it will come back.'"

That gave me a lot to ponder on.

When we returned home we watched from the backyard as the summer sun slowly sank and painted the sky a red-orange. I grilled steaks and foil-wrapped potatoes and Ginger had made a wonderful spinach salad. We relaxed side-by-side in lounge chairs, pleasantly tired, and relaxed from a bottle of wine. Birds twittered as they flitted from branch to branch in the neighborhood trees. The remnants of our dinner cluttered the picnic table.

Suddenly Ginger reached for my hand and squeezed it softly. When I turned to look at her, her expression was one of pure love. She nodded her head towards the house, got up, and went inside. Something stirred in my heart. I followed her upstairs.

My body was excited; it had been a while since I'd had sex with Lynn and I'd had countless fantasies about what it would be like with Ginger.

As the door closed behind us, our bodies surrendered to a deep passion. No more fantasies; it was really about to happen. We embraced, kissing deeply, and tore each other's clothes off, as we explored every crevice of each other's body. Time stood still. Each breath brought us closer until we became one. Months of sexual energy had built up in both of us, and was released simultaneously. I looked down into her eyes and it felt so right to be making love with her. Suddenly three words came out of my mouth that I've never uttered before: "I love you."

It was a wonderful weekend. Richard saw his first live baseball game, and I got some good exercise. Ginger and I made love several times, even once in the kitchen while our kids played in the yard. But most importantly, I had begun to see some light shine into my life.

Sam called me at exactly 9:00 a.m. on Tuesday. "Good morning, Scott," he said vigorously.

"What's up, Sam?"

"I've got some good news for you, sonny. What's on your calendar for Wednesday morning?"

"It's open."

"Good. Do you play golf?"

"Sure," I acknowledged confidently, "but I can use a little practice."

"Fine, then. I'll reserve an early tee-off at my country club."

I was excited. Golf on a work day with Sam — what a way to go! "Hey, Sam. About what time will we be teeing-off?"

"I'll try for 6:30 a.m."

"Isn't that kind of early?"

"Not really, Scott. Ed Vernan needs to be back for a twelve o'clock meeting."

I was stunned, My body cringed and my heart beat rapidly. Sweat broke out on my hands. "Vernan's coming?" I timidly asked. I heard Sam chuckle in the background. One round of golf, or more accurately, groping with Ginger hadn't prepared me for that.

"It's an opportunity," Sam said eagerly.

Wednesday morning arrived before I knew it. At four a.m. the sun doesn't shine, nor do the eyes open. But for a nervous grunt who didn't get much sleep, the battle was just beginning. I met Sam and Ed at six o'clock sharp by the Pro Shop. They were both well-outfitted in white golf attire and my baggy khaki pants were no match for the occasion. If it hadn't been for Sam, I would have forgotten to rent clubs. In spite of the warm morning breeze, my body was already soaked with perspiration.

Our call came at 6:30 and I had the honor of teeing-off first. My face was frozen in a weak smile, and my hands grasped the club so tightly that the pattern on the grip was impressed in my skin. I closed my eyes as I lifted my club. Just as I took a swing., the image of Ginger bending over in a short skirt flashed into my mind.

The whooshing of empty air was not what was expected. Vernan grunted. I wanted to die right then and there as the ball stared back at me in disgust from its perch on the green. One more try resulted in a squish-clunk. The damn ball bounced itself off the tee about thirty yards onto the fairway.

Vernan's ball sailed 190 yards. Sam beat that by at least twenty yards. Blood rushed into my head and I thought I'd explode with embarrassment. I couldn't exhale. My life ended on the first green. Why had I been such a fool as to get suckered into this?

Sam suggested that I take a couple of deep breaths before the next swing. He also recommended that I use a one iron.

As the massacre continued, I began mentally drafting a suicide note. On the third hole, Vernan approached me and said, "Damn it, Scott, don't be so nervous. It's only a game!"

Easy for you to say, I thought. Your entire future isn't on the line. This was my judgment day, and my corporate god was getting visibly irritated by how I was slowing his game down.

My next shot was good, a solid and straight eighty yards. Hope rang through my body.

Vernan came up to me again and said, "If you played golf as well and as hard as you work, Sam and I would be trying to catch up with you."

My next shot went out an easy 150 yards but suddenly hooked sharply and forever disappeared into the rough, taking my career with it.

"We'll get you to shoot par," Sam said, "but it's going to take a lot of practice."

"You can count on me," I said.

To which Vernan added, "Son, hard work never failed a man and commitment is what makes a man successful."

I thought those excellent words. They should be written in a business management textbook. Perhaps Vernan could be a mentor to me. Everything he said made sense, and we began to talk more openly about the virtues of becoming a consistent golfer. Somehow our conversation moved from the golf course to the office, and Vernan kept bringing up corporate activities, which I wanted to know more about.

By the time we reached the sixteenth green, I was hitting no more than four over par, per hole. Our conversations focused on marketing strategies and recruiting college graduates in computer science, business administration, and marketing. Sam and I had a moment alone and he commented on how easily Vernan could influence me. He prodded me to take a stand on issues, just to let Vernan know I was not a push-over. Frankly, I was getting annoyed at Sam for bugging me but what had Sam suggested made sense. However, I was on overload, overwhelmed with input, dialog, and a frustrating game.

After the game, Sam treated us to a delicious early lunch at the club. I had to put up with their relentless teasing about my pitiful putting and high score.

While we were polishing off our desert, Vernan asked me out of the blue, "Scott, my lad, where do you see yourself at CSC in the future?"

Sam looked intensely at me and shook his head almost imperceptibly as if to warn, "Think on this for a minute."

But caution flew out the window as the opportunity to tell Vernan my ultimate ambition took center stage. Everything I'd ever dreamed of and worked so hard to achieve welled up in me. "I'd like to be a vice president," I announced proudly.

Sam cringed and Vernan scrutinized me carefully. I was astounded how much his eyes, his manner, reminded me of my father at that moment. "You would, huh?" he said derisively. "Just like that? Why vice president? Why not president?"

His words caused time run to backwards.

I was nine years old and helping my father out in the bank one day during the summer. I hated it because in his eyes, I could never do anything right. This particular day there was a stack of folders that needed filing. Every half hour or so he would stop whatever he was doing and check the file cabinet to make sure I hadn't misfiled anything. I was so afraid of making a mistake that my progress was slow. I knew the alphabet but names like MacGovern or McGillvary always messed me up.

As my father thumbed through the files, he yanked out one folder, then another, and then another. "MacCormack comes before McCormick!" he said angrily. "I swear, you'll never amount to anything if you don't get your priorities straight. I won't always be behind you to clean up your mess. When I was your age, I was a full-time file clerk here during summer vacations. There wasn't anyone to check on my work. I had to get it right the first time or lose my job."

Hurt and angry, I blurted out, "Then how come you're not the president of the bank by now?"

My father's body tensed and the loudest silence I'd ever heard reverberated through the cluttered office. The monotonous tick of the second hand on the wall clock was a time bomb, each tick bringing me that much closer to his explosive anger.

He took a deep breath and then turned around and whipped his open hand across the side of my head, knocking me to the tiled floor. He towered above me, his legs spread wide, his eyes narrowed, his face twisted with disgust. "Listen, you wise-ass," he said through clenched teeth, punctuating each word with an enormous finger pointed at me, "don't ever let me hear you mock me again. My sweat from this shitty job puts the food in your mouth and the clothes on your back. The day you become the president of a big corporation—even a *vice* president— then you'll have earned the right to be my son, but not until then."

When I came back to the present, Sam and Vernan were gone. I was totally alone at the table with only dirty dishes to help me sort out my tangled thoughts.

I took a sip of ice water, too stunned at the vision of my repressed memory to think clearly. Anger and pain momentarily roared through me. If my father had walked in right then, I would have decked him. Mentally, I did. A lifetime of repression would have powered a punch that would have knocked him through the wall. I saw him lying on the carpeted floor near my table at the prestigious country club, with me standing over him saying, "I have nothing to prove to you. How you feel about me is your problem." At that moment, I saw the wisdom of my unsaid words and felt a surge of euphoric freedom.

During my solitary ride to the office, I replayed all the morning's conversations. I'd felt shitty when the day began and, ironically, after a marvelous time on the golf course, I felt even shittier.

There was a message in my electronic mail from Sam that said: "The Indian warrior told the chief he wanted to become the chief. The chief had him slain."

I called Sam. "I guess I blew it, huh?"

"I saw it coming," Sam said. "All you had to do was to let Vernan act out his creativity, let him suggest what you should be in his organization. He eats that up. Instead, *you* told him."

"What are you really trying to tell me, Sam?"

"No way in hell am I going to give you that answer, my friend. It's about time you start thinking before you totally destroy yourself."

I pondered Sam's challenge for the rest of the afternoon. I managed to get my mind and body back home at the end of the day. A nice cold beer and some leftover chili soothed my aching body and chaotic thoughts. I refused to think about my father. I was aware that something in me had shifted but I didn't know what.

By 8:30 I was stretched out in bed and easily drifted away. I saw Kama's face. Her long, wavy red hair surrounded me. Her unique and beautiful personality glowed. We began to talk and she told me how happy she was with her job, her travels, her new home. We laughed as we walked upstairs to her bedroom overlooking the magnificent Pacific. She moved closer to me and I wanted to kiss her. I closed my eyes and felt her soft lips pressing against mine. We kissed long and deeply, merging our souls into one.

In our flight, her face began to slowly change. I tried to tell her how much I loved her. She kept saying that she loved me but she slowly faded away. As my heart reached out to her, her voice and eyes came back to me as Lynn. I wanted to kiss her. I closed my eyes and felt her soft lips. We kissed and love once again embraced our souls. But then her face changed into the face of Ginger, and our souls wove into a braid as the dream ended.

Chapter 17

SQUASH

I woke up sweating over the dream in which Kama, Lynn, and Ginger merged into one woman who loved me so deeply that it hurt. With my mind still racing, I sat up in bed and realized that three women truly and deeply loved me, and I had let two of them go. For the first time I could remember, I cried. The true horror of losing love like that began to dawn on me, and I spiraled down into wretched despair.

At nine, I had barely enough energy to call the office.

"Good morning, this is Maria. How may I help you?"

"Hey, Maria. It's Scott. Listen, mark me down for a sick day. Actually, a mental health day. Okay?"

"Honey, are you okay? Do you want me to do anything for you?"

"No. Thanks anyway. I need some time for myself."

"I understand," she said.

I went downstairs to make a pot of coffee but I spooned instant in a cup instead. Eggs and bacon seemed like too much work. A bowl of Cheerios sufficed. I was in the midst of talking idiotically to the little circles of oats floating in my bowl when I remembered to get the morning papers. As I walked through the barren, lifeless house I felt the absence of Lynn as an actual physical pain. A deep loneliness washed over me.

The headlines stared up at me as I opened the door. More negative bullshit. I slammed the door shut, leaving the paper to the sprinkler system. My reunion with the Cheerio family was soggy. I abandoned them as I had my own family and went back to bed.

Waking up at three in the afternoon erased all sense of time and direction. I felt as if I'd died and then woken up on another planet. I was hungry and made the trip to the kitchen again. The voyage was successful. A couple of slices of bread separated by bologna furnished my taste buds with temporary joy. The sight of a full bag of potato chips made me instantly sick, reminding me of that ill-fated day when I had bombed out with my family.

With the rest of my sandwich in hand, I strolled out into the yard. I noticed Lynn's special garden hoe leaning on the fence. I saw her putting it away in the shed. She turned to me, offered me a smile, then disappeared. The yard was haunted. I went back into the house.

I saw Richard running by me as I headed upstairs. His laugh killed me.

The pillow around my face was cool and comforting. I lay there crying, knowing quite well that those I loved left my life because I had chased them away. Kama and Lynn were wonderful beings who had wanted to share their lives with me, and all I'd done was trample on their love and finally reject it. And at the thought that I might do the same to Ginger, I broke down into uncontrollable sobs and cried myself to sleep.

I awoke the next day feeling calm, clear, and almost perky.

The ride up the elevator was swift. As the door opened, Maria spotted me. "Are you okay, Scott?" she inquired, her face cheerful and open.

"I feel fine today," I said, and on impulse, hugged her. Then I backed up and said, "But yesterday was a disaster."

I grabbed a cup of coffee on the way to the office. Sitting back in my chair, I continued to reflect on some of the situations that surrounded me since I had begun working at CSC. Then I chuckled. Here I was, sitting around doing absolutely nothing productive, and it was okay. Five years ago, I was literally killing myself to get ahead. Boy, Scott, I thought, you really have come far: no family and no vice presidency. I had tried so hard, had worked such long hours, including weekends. Rarely did I take a sick day. Always on time, always loyal serving the company, always respecting my superiors. What a disappointment I was. But now I knew that working within the system was easier than trying to improve it. Making up with Maria was a perfect example. So why did I graduate from college thinking I could change the world?

I turned to my desktop friend and the e-mail went into action. Sam wanted to see me. I called him first.

"Hi, Sam. It's me, Scott. What's up?"

"We need to organize some things for the retirement party. Can you come up for an hour or so?"

"Yeah, sure. Why not?"

It only took twenty minutes to accomplish our agenda. Sam had been acting put-off since the luncheon at his country club. It bothered me, so I confronted him. "Sam, be honest with me. Something's bugging you and I think it's me. Can you give me a clue?"

He reached for his old friend, the pipe.

"Does it have any thing to do with Vernan?" I prodded.

He didn't respond until his third puff. Then he said, "Yep. Sure does. There's a lot I want to say to you, Scott."

Slightly annoyed yet ready for combat, I snapped, "Then let's have it!"

"Since I first met you, I sensed your need to get tougher with yourself. You know, to be more of a man. Confident. Do you follow me?"

I nodded. I knew he was right.

"Over several weeks," Sam continued, "I've gathered some interesting information about you. You're bright, highly energetic, too damn ambitious, and very ignorant about people and life in general. Was your upbringing difficult?"

"No, not really, but it was boring. My dad worked in a bank as a loan officer. He constantly bitched about his job, especially about how his boss kept holding him back."

"I see," Sam said. "What about your mother?"

"She was a typical martyr, a complaining woman. She waited on my dad and me hand and foot, literally. But it came with a price. She complained the whole time."

"Did she have a job?"

"She was a housewife and mother all of the time. My father wouldn't let her work. It demeaned him somehow."

"What did the family do as a whole? You know, fun stuff."

"Television was just about it. Once in a while, dad got the urge to go sight-seeing. He took us once to the Statue of Liberty and the Empire State Building. The beach was his favorite place. Usually, it was television that occupied most of our time at night and on weekends. I loved to watch basketball but dad loved to watch football."

"Hmmm," Sam said. "Were your parents happy about you going to college?"

"They didn't seem to care much, one way or the other. When I told them I was going to go, they wanted me to go to a local college but I wanted to get away from home. I played pretty much the first year. First time away from home, and all. Then I figured that some day college would make me rich and famous."

"I see. Tell me more about that if you want to, Scott."

"Sure, why not. You see, my dad never went to college. He believed that his career in the bank was stifled by the fact that he worked there most of his life but he didn't have a college degree. I don't know much about his early life because he never talked about it. He was pretty much of an explosive man when he got angry about something. In his eyes, I never amounted to much. Maybe he said it so much I began to believe it."

"I see," Sam said thoughtfully.

"You know, when Vernan asked me what I wanted to be in the company, I experienced a flashback to when I was a kid. I was nine years old, filing some reports for my father in the bank one day, and I made a mistake. He knocked me to the floor and told me that I would never be his son until I became the president, or even a vice president, of a big corporation."

"A self-fulfilling prophecy," Sam said, puffing blue smoke into the room. "Well, Scott, you definitely had a reason to set a goal, even if it was self-defeating. But now I have to inform you of something that you may not like but must learn to accept."

Sam's rigid posture meant trouble. "Vernan doesn't feel that you've got a strong enough personality for corporate management. He likes you—that's good—but when you told him about wanting to be a vice president, you instantly turned him off."

"So easily?"

"Do you want an IF statement? IF you'd said to Vernan, 'Do you see me as a vice president?' he would have been more receptive to you. You see, Scott, people who are successful around Vernan give him the opportunity to think. Whenever somebody tries to *tell* him something, he usually reacts by closing down."

"So telling him that I wanted to be a vice president was asking for rejection?" I was beginning to understand.

"Hey, son, you're listening. Keep that up and you'll see some progress."

"Tell me, Sam, how do you talk to Vernan?"

"Very carefully. And when I do, it's eye-to-eye. I look at him straight-away and state my view, but leave him plenty of room to state his view. This is something you must learn if you are to succeed with people."

On that note, I made my way back to my office. Sam, in his usual fashion, had prompted some critical thinking and that's what I did. I needed to know more about the corporate game in order to survive in it.

Over the next three months, I began to see a lot more of Ginger and her daughter, Christy. Eventually, Richard spent most of the weekends with the three of us. Sometimes it was a bit tense. Two children made it difficult for Ginger and I to be alone, but after we were sure they were asleep, Ginger and I would cuddle up on the sofa and usually end up making love. It was a family in the making.

I also did a lot of thinking about my failed marriage with Lynn, my job, and my life in general. I slowed down a bit but I still found myself unsettled with who I was and with the issues surrounding me. I put the final touches on Sam's retirement ceremony and made sure that all my projects were completed in an excellent and timely fashion.

Ed Vernan's opinion of me kept prodding at my conscious mind. He had labeled me. College doesn't teach anything about the real world with all it unwritten rules such as how to avoid being labeled, learning the system of politicking, being aware of nasty self-serving predators, learning how to confront and stand firm, seeking the truth. College teaches theories like who said this and who said that. Graduates are inadequately prepared to meet the world with abstract thoughts that don't have any meaning in real life.

Lynn officially said good-bye; the divorce was final. There's one thing Lynn taught me well: once trust leaves a relationship, the relationship is over. Once she truly believed that I had approached another woman for comfort, there was no recourse. Love was of no matter to Lynn once the trust was gone. And it was my arrogant determination that my career should dominate three lives that had chased Lynn's trust away.

Chapter 18

THE DEATH OF A MULE

The long-awaited moment arrived. Tom came into my room and announced my promotion to division manager. I was to be Tom's replacement, resulting from his own promotion to director of data processing earlier that year. I was elated. I now had a secretary of my own, one assistant, and twenty-two people to supervise.

It had taken me seven years to reach this level. God only knew how long it was going to take to reach the top. Despite everything, I had made it this far. I would now be moving into a bigger office, one with a window. Tom now occupied the large office next to Ira's suite.

I should have shown more excitement, but it was anti-climactic. In the past six months, I'd finally found some peace and had control over some of my projects. Now, because of my promotion, I would be starting all over again. More work, more people, more games, even a new family. I sensed that my second life was just beginning and that scared me silly.

One day Ben walked into my office, cocky and exuberant. "Wow, Scott, you've finally reached middle management."

"Yeah. I'm already working a few hours extra."

"Hey, my friend, this is what you wanted. You got what you said was important to you, so enjoy the glory it brings. Just remember, you create your own future."

"Okay. What brings you here today?"

"I'm leaving CSC."

"You're *what*?"

"I've given it a lot of thought, Scott, and I feel great about my decision."

"What does the future hold for you, Ben?"

"Kama," he grinned.

My mouth dropped open. "Kama?"

"Yes, Kama. We're gonna get married."

"You're kidding me, Ben."

"Not this time, Scott. I love her and she loves me. I'm leaving for San Francisco in thirty days. We're going to have a wedding in a small chapel in Napa Valley. I'd like you to be my best man. Both Kama and I know you and love you. We want you to be a part of this happy occasion."

I froze, cottonmouth and all. Then a smile snuck onto my face. "Sure, Ben. I'd love to be your best man. "

I called Kama to offer my congratulations. I was nervous and still a little jealous, but I had to speak with her.

"Good morning! Shasta Computer Systems. May I help you?"

"I'd like to speak with Kama Rowley."

"Thank you. I'll connect you."

"Good morning," a mature woman's voice acknowledged, "this is Brenda Rodriguez speaking. May I help you?"

"I'm trying to reach Kama Rowley," I said with annoyance. I didn't want to speak to anyone but Kama.

"Is this a business or a personal call?"

"Business," I snapped.

"Your name, please?"

"Scott Hendrick."

"What firm do you represent, Mr. Hendrick?"

"CSC."

"Just one moment, please."

While waiting, I wondered what was so difficult. All I wanted to do was talk to Kama.

"Thank you for waiting, Mr. Hendrick. Miss Rowley will be happy to speak with you. Can you hold?"

"Yes." Curious about the long-winded introductions, I asked Brenda why all the fuss before she put me on hold.

She was surprised by my inquiry. "I'm Miss Rowley's executive assistant. We get so many calls, I do my best to screen them."

I was stunned. I asked for clarification.

"Oh, I thought you knew, Mr. Hendrick. Miss Rowley is our senior vice president."

With that I grunted and swallowed. "Senior vice president?"

"Yes, sir. She's ready for you now, Mister Hendrick."

"Scotty! How are you?" Kama said enthusiastically.

"I'm really fine, thank you." Kama sounded great.

"Ben talks a lot about you, Scott."

"Anything bad?"

"Just that you're still knocking yourself out, trying to do your best."

"Yeah, but I've finally got things under control. I've been promoted to Division Manager, Tom's old position."

"Yes, I know. Ben told me. Congratulations!"

"So, Kama, what's this about your new position?"

"It's amazing, Scott. I'm in love with this company. They're all a bunch of great people out here. I wish you would come out and be part of the crew."

"Maybe in the future. Right now I'm settled in for a while. You know, the new job, Richard, and all that."

"Are you sure you don't want to give it a try?"

"Like I said, CSC is finally delivering. What's it like being at the top?"

"Not quite at the top, but it's really a great feeling, totally different than I ever imagined."

"How did it happen so fast?"

"I created many opportunities for client expansion. We all work as a team here, especially in my former position as technical consultant. Eventually, I emerged as a leader. I got a few extra bucks, more resources to free me up, and—whammo—I started to really do the things I felt would make the company grow, that would increase client satisfaction."

"How on earth did you pull that off? I mean, wasn't it difficult to persuade your bosses?"

"Once I was convinced that corporate people are simply people who need to be motivated, I felt more at ease with them. After ridding myself of that bullshit bureaucratic mentality at CSC, I turned that energy into creative activity. It gave me confidence. I tried a few things here and there. Some worked, some didn't. But overall, I started to roll. I generated a couple million dollars of revenue, which yielded substantial profits. We all worked harder and longer, but boy, we played, too!

"It's kind of funny, Scotty, but I rarely thought about advancing or getting promoted. I focused most of my energies on feeling good about myself, as well as the tasks that lay ahead of me. Promotions came as a result of my love for the job and respect for my peers and superiors."

"How did the V.P. position come about?"

"The president of the company asked me if I would be interested in developing a formal proposal for him to present to the Board Members. He wanted to create a new department and needed my expertise and insight on how that could evolve. Of course, I was honored."

"And?"

"The Board approved the proposal. Soon afterwards, I became head of the department, which was successful, and was offered more recognition. So now I am senior vice president of Shasta. Isn't that great?"

Kama shared many good things with me. She explained how Shasta would hold a monthly meeting to reinforce its position on the company's philosophy and policies. Shasta believed that long-term success was predicated on excellent customer service, effective corporate humanity, and continued employee growth. Generating a positive attitude would inevitably produce the talent and creativity needed for continued success in the marketplace.

She also gave me insight on how, by contrast, CSC sought to earn short-term profits in order to satisfy quarterly reports. With this short-term mentality, whatever it took to look good for the quarter became the accepted standard of management.

Management consistency and inspiration are needed to build an effective and productive work force, she said. When management loses its ability to collaboratively achieve its goals and productivity, then it becomes separated from the work force. Corporate vision is then replaced by closed-mindedness, pressure, and fear. Eventually, the majority of employees become isolated and apathetic, and cease being accountable for their work.

Our conversation was very inspiring. I felt nothing but happiness and joy for Kama. We spoke for an hour and felt closer to each other than ever before.

The time for Sam Hawkins' retirement finally arrived. Actually, it was a big event for me, too. After all, with his encouragement, I did most of the planning and organizing of the ceremony, which meant a lot of running around, checking, and double-checking. Nonetheless, the night arrived for over a hundred of Sam's friends and, most deservingly, Sam Hawkins himself.

CEO John Mayes led off with a rehearsed speech. Ed Vernan followed with a ceremonial toasting of his long-time friend. Ira Eastman presented his boring version of humor. I was, of course, the host.

The dinner at a downtown hotel was excellent and the mood was quite upbeat for such an occasion. All tables had bouquets of fresh flowers and were dressed in the finest china. I had the privilege of saying a few words in his honor, words that were well received. Then Sam stepped up to the podium. He began a most tactful and articulate speech. I was amazed at his never-ending talents. His friends cheered him on. His topic concerned the mystery of the workplace and how he had survived in it.

At one point, he paused for a full fifteen seconds until the guests became quiet and attentive. When the entire room, hotel staff included, became silent, he offered a final comment.

"I don't know how you all feel in regards to reincarnation or whatever they call it, but in my next life, if I should have a chance, I know one thing for sure: I'm not going to slave like a mule for anyone else's dream. Instead, I'll be what I want to be. When you look back at it all, it's not what you *have* that counts cuz ya can't take it with you, anyway. It's who you *are*, how great you feel, and most importantly, how *free* you want to be."

He got a standing ovation. There were tears in my eyes. Even the CEO applauded wholeheartedly.

Sam's words made me think a lot about freedom. How can you find freedom in a corporate setting like CSC? Is it even possible?

Maybe as Janice Joplin sings, "Freedom's just another word for nothing left to lose." Maybe it's our attachments to people, places, and things that rob us of our freedom. Attachment to something brings anxiety about losing it. Did my attachment to being a vice president rob me of my freedom? If I dropped the attachment, would I be free?

The years rolled by. I missed having Ben and Sam around, although we kept in touch. My job became ordinary. I easily fell into the ranks of corporate bureaucracy. I wrote memos, kept costs down, attended meetings, supervised my department, and on and on.

I often thought about Kama attaining such a high level corporate position. My wish to be a vice president still occupies my mind, even though I don't feel that I have to prove myself to my father—or myself—any longer. Why in hell would I want to be a V.P. now? Maybe because it's been such a dream for so long that it's hard to part with it. It's become part of who I am.

Life seemed to be one gigantic reflection of the past. What should I have done? What if? If only I knew how to face life in the moment. I find myself reacting to most of my thoughts. Sometimes I feel that my gut instinct tries to tell me to do something else but *trusting* it is difficult for me. Could that be my problem?

I remember something Sam once said to me: "Your journey toward success is through learning. When an event presents itself and you fail to learn from it, it will return. Therefore, learning is your opportunity to know more about yourself, your relationships, and the world you have chosen to live in. If you put an ounce of love into what you learn, then you'll become happier as a person. You'll begin to see that what you do today, does indeed, create your tomorrow. When you see your own face, it will be more peaceful."

Ginger has already helped me to live more in the moment. Her love of nature and the simple pleasures in life are beginning to rub off on me. I'd always thought that things like holding hands in the moonlight were songwriters' clichés, but when they thrill Ginger, I can't help but stop and enjoy the moment, too.

Allowing her to love me without me thinking that her love poses an obligation, that I must do something in response other than receive it, has been a major step. Lynn telling me she loved me always put me on the defensive. With Ginger, I just let it in. Maybe one day, I'll really understand.

In the meantime, I'll keep plugging away. There will be opportunities ahead for me, maybe even a chance for me to become a vice president at CSC.

Epilogue

THE TRANSITION

Many years passed. Kama's quest for a work environment that recognized individual creativity and encouraged self-expression. Her position was based on cooperation rather than competition paid off and she was promoted to president of her company. Under her leadership, its profits went through the roof and she became a very wealthy woman.

Ben became a tenured professor in the Department of Organizational Psychology at UC Berkeley. Kama and Ben remained happily married and had three daughters.

Lynn earned her Ph.D. at Georgia State and became a renowned consultant in her field. To my surprise, I had some reservations about her becoming involved with other men. Sam got a part-time job in the pro shop of his country club. Eventually, the grand old man opened up a pipe craft shop.

Ginger and I got married and I adopted Christy as my child. Richard went off to college in Washington to study Environmental Geophysics. He wanted nothing to do with the corporate business world.

For me at CSC, the world of corporate glamour grew quite stale. It no longer excited me. All those dedicated years and for what? Corporate profits fluctuated, as did the mood of management.

One day, twelve Japanese investors visited CSC and wanted to survey our computer programming methods. In actuality, they appeared more curious about how the company operated. This started some speculation, but when a rumor hit the grapevine about a merger with a leading competitor, tension was everywhere. Someone said that management had planted the rumor, but then management quickly denied the rumor. Too quickly, everyone thought. No-one knew what was true anymore, and small, impromptu gatherings in the hall-ways became normal.

I was amazed at how peers and friends began to compete and position themselves for the eventual merger. Ego games and power-tripping flourished in middle management. Chaos prevailed. I still held onto my dream of becoming a vice presi-dent even as my life at CSC rapidly collapsed all around me.

The final blow came when the president sent down a memo announcing that the Japanese software company, Yishito, had bought CSC. The memo warned of downsizing and layoffs, because the Japanese didn't like corporate fat or do-nothing management. The axe would soon hang over all our heads. Who was to be slain and who was to be saved? All hell broke loose. I felt like a martyr dying for nothing.

When I got home, Ginger was in the kitchen preparing sup-per. "Hi, babe," I called out as I entered through the back door.

"Good news from your Aunt Anne in Arizona, hon!" she shouted. "She'd love to have you visit her."

"That's exactly what I need, some good news. Maybe I should go to Arizona, dig a big hole in the desert, and climb in."

"You sound pretty down, Scotty. Is everything okay?"

"Not at all okay. The Japanese bought CSC. The memo was issued today."

Without hesitation, Ginger rushed to my side. "It will all work out for the best, sweetheart."

"Oh, sure it will. What about my promotion? What about my lifetime of service? Who'll give a damn?"

"So when is the takeover going to happen?"

"By the end of the month."

"So fast?"

"My guess is that a lot of heads are going to roll, including mine. CSC has been riding quite high on the hog with over-head. I'll bet you that tomorrow will be a sad day at the office.

Maria, bless her soul, probably knows what the hell's going on. I'll give her a call after dinner."

By nine, I'd finished a two-hour conversation with Maria. My ear was hot and my stomach turbulent. It was now evident that my dreams were shattered. The Japanese prefer flat hierarchies and two whole layers of middle management had been axed, including my job, of course.

After two days of restless suspense, I finally received the inevitable it's-time-to-go notice. I sat in my office for an hour, staring at the walls and reflecting on everything that I'd accomplished at CSC. I relived twenty years of pep talks, manipulation for advancement, all the hard work. For what? I'd been circumcised once again.

I called Ginger at home. "Hi, sweetheart. I got the early retirement package." I could hear her crying and tried to console her a bit. "Despite all the shit, Ginger, they've offered me a very lucrative deal that gives me plenty of time to look around. It'll be okay, sweetheart."

I worked on my resume and had several interviews with professional head-hunters but I was anxious to leave CSC. That was a strange feeling to experience. Departure day came and several of us went out to lunch and got pretty drunk.

We started lunch with boisterous bids to out do each other's war stories about how bad working at CSC had been. Then we moved into cynicism about the extremely generous golden handshakes senior management had received, Maria, of course, providing the details.

Two more rounds of drinks saw us dissecting senior management's sex lives and who was screwing who in the executive offices, again with Maria providing the lurid details.

By three o'clock, the reality had set in for me that on Monday morning, I would no longer be part of Atlanta's bustling business community. No assigned parking place, no window office, and certainly no shot at a vice presidency. What had it all been for, I wondered. Kama once told me that she believed in reincarnation, and that we set up each life for a specific purpose. If that was true, I thought, what had I intended to achieve in this lifetime, and was I succeeding?

My reverie was interrupted when a glass of cold beer accidentally fell off an overcrowded table into my lap. What surprised me was that I really didn't care.

Sitting at home doing nothing bothered me. I was restless and bitter about CSC's takeover. I kept thinking about my life with all that devotion and hard work at CSC. It didn't make sense to me. How can companies do this to their employees? I really took it personally and became more and more bitter.

Tension also rose at home. Ginger and Christy tried their best to calm me down. It was getting uncomfortable and the stress was mounting for everybody. Ginger finally urged me to take advantage of Aunt Anne's offer. I agreed. I packed and drove cross-country to Flagstaff, Arizona.

Aunt Anne was a radiant doll. She was a silver-haired lady who was as healthy as a horse. She looked at life in a positive and upbeat manner and she wouldn't permit me to feel sorry for myself in her presence. She was tough, spunky, and alert–more than I could say for myself.

"Get out there, boy! Enjoy nature. Climb a mountain," she would tell me vigorously. So, one morning, she packed a picnic basket full of goodies and pushed me out the door. I couldn't refuse so I went off toward the hills. The drive was fabulous, and the red canyons and cliffs around Sedona were beautiful.

Life was free and easy out in the West. It brought me a feeling of freedom I hadn't felt since I was a child. Nature has its ways, I guess.

I drove through the small town of Cottonwood and stopped to buy gas at the station opposite a fine old bank building. The carved inscription over the doors read, " 1893." Over a hundred years, I thought. As I gazed at the building, I had the weird feeling that I'd been here before. I chuckled—I'd never been to Arizona in my life.

As I drove out of Cottonwood, I approached a scenic overlook. I pulled over, got out of the car, and walked over to the edge of the cliff to take a look. The canyon and the valley below were breathtaking. A breeze streamed through me as though I was transparent. It was heaven. My body twitched and shivered as if something tingled in every part of me. I felt alive for the first time in years.

I drove down into the valley and noticed how green and open everything was. Most of the people were ranchers and wore cowboy hats and jeans. They were hearty, rugged, and tanned. I liked what I saw.

As I started up the canyon road, I noticed a sign that said, "MULE RANCH FOR SALE." The "$25,000 DOWN" caught my eye, so I pulled in to take a look. As I walked towards the gate, something strange happened. A blissful sensation filled me as I scanned the ranch with its herd of scattered draft mules and the surrounding canyons. It felt like home, like I'd been here before.

I went back to the car, grabbed the picnic basket, and walked along the dirt road to the ranch. It was quiet, deserted, and lined with an array of trees. The view all around was gorgeous, immeasurably more beautiful than what I had seen from the rim of the canyon. I found an overlook and a place to sit. Still dazed by the peace and calm about me, I enjoyed Aunt Anne's wonderful lunch. I felt better sitting there alone than I could recall ever feeling in my entire life. CSC, Lynn, money, and my old dreams no longer mattered. For perhaps the first time in my life, I felt really happy.

Everything that Ben, Kama, and Sam had tried to drum into my stubborn skull suddenly became clear. An uncontrollable sobbing welled up from somewhere deep within me. I knew then that I'd given up my soul for causes that were not mine. Tears ran down my face as I realized that I'd been waiting for life to come to me. I realized that rather than living a life filled with love and happiness, I'd spent my entire life pursuing something that was totally meaningless. I realized, too, that my heart and soul needed love.

As my thoughts and emotions raced through and around me, I collapsed under a tree and fell asleep. I woke up cold and hungry under the most magnificent starlit night imaginable. I was overwhelmed with joy. Every fiber in my body felt rejuvenated and complete.

I scurried back to the car, turned on the heater, and drove to the first public phone I found on the side of the road. "Ginger! Ginger, it's me. Ginger, darling, we're going to buy a mule ranch. We're going to LIVE life. I'm the luckiest guy in the world! I really, really love you!"

Ginger responded with an exuberant cry of "Yes, yes, YES!"

Aunt Anne was my guardian angel. Her smile and warmth were filled with compassion and wisdom. She became the center of our family and a resident of our new home, *The Happy Mule Ranch.*

Christy took care of the mules and loved riding her horse in and around the canyons. Richard visited often from his home in California, usually with a beautiful girlfriend in tow. He was surprisingly well-adjusted after such a turbulent childhood, thanks mainly to Lynn's strength of character. He and I would take long walks around the canyons, talking about our lives and what we'd learned. He once told me that the greatest gift I'd given him was an example of how he *didn't* want his life to be. He said that with such gratitude in his voice that I must have hugged him for over a minute, tears streaming down my face. Ben and Kama would have been proud of me, I thought fleetingly.

Ginger opened up a bed and breakfast on the ranch and found her true forte as a gracious hostess. The folks out West certainly seemed to enjoy her Southern cooking and hospitality.

I've come to like the town of Cottonwood, with its feed and grain merchants and the general store. And I feel really secure with the bank. After all, they've had only one robbery, and that was a hundred years ago!

As for me, I'd sum it up this way: From now on, I'm going to live *my* dreams and *my* goals. I'd spent a lifetime jumping through hoops like a trained animal for other people's goals, my father's especially.

Everyday I give thanks that I had found out, before it was too late, what's truly important: love, the smile of a woman who loves you, a warm pat on the back from a son who likes and respects you, and daily miracles like the birth of a new foal.

I still shake my head in wonder at the poor Scott who would work twelve-hour days in a tiny, windowless office, chasing illusions while the important things in life passed him by. Maybe Kama was right. Maybe discovering all this was what this lifetime has been about.

But I know one thing: Never again will I give up my soul for someone else's goal.

THE CORPORATE MULE HUMANE SOCIETY

Many people who have read *The Corporate Mule* have shared their stories with us. It's amazing how many of us, in some manner, have experienced a scenario similar to the one fictitiously depicted in this book.

As a matter of service to the readers, the publisher has agreed to publish another book and eventually set up the "Never Again Corporate Mule Society."

Our second book, for the most part, will be a collection of short stories received from our readers. These true short stories will reflect their experiences: what happened, the event's outcomes, and lessons learned from their corporate experiences.

The book will be titled *The Corporate Mule Humane Society— A Collection of True Stories About the Workplace.*

All authors selected will share proportionately in any royalties earned from sales of the book. If you have a story you want to tell, please submit it in both hardcopy and on a floppy disk (Word or WordPerfect for IBM-compatible or Mac). Stories should be 1,500 words or less, double-spaced, edited and proofed as best you can, and accompanied by a $25 processing fee, payable to Oughten House Publications. Make sure your name appears on every page, and number the pages.

See our web site, www.oughtenhouse.com for details and information for entry rules, selection criteria, names of literary judges, list of author selections, and information about the "Never Again Corporate Mule Society."

All authors selected will be notified by mail and will be required to sign appropriate publishing contracts. Please forward to:

"The Corporate Mule Humane Society"
Oughten House Publications
P.O. Box 2008
Livermore, CA 94551-2008 USA
No phone calls please. All entries due by November 30, 1997.

ABOUT THE AUTHOR

Robert Vincent Gerard began his working career as a civil engineer. Finding his interests lay with people, not things, he went back to college and completed a Bachelor's Degree in Social Psychology (1978), a Master's Degree in Management and Organizational Psychology (1981), and the required course work for a doctorate in Educational Management at Georgia State University, and Spiritual Psychology at the California Institute of Integral Studies. He then worked as an Organizational Consultant and Corporate Consultant specializing in improving communication and resolving conflicts within entire companies. His methods for the creative handling of confrontations eventually found their way into written form, with the current working title of *Handling Verbal Confrontations: Taking the Fear Out of Facing Others.*

Gerard's first published book emerged in 1988 under the title *Shar Dae, Empress of Peace.* In 1992, Gerard founded Oughten House Publications, which has become a world leader in books and materials dedicated to supporting the rising planetary consciousness in all its forms. *Shar Dae* was extensively revised and published under the Oughten House imprint in 1995 as *Lady From Atlantis.* Gerard has since founded Oughten House Foundation and is currently expanding it to offer assistance to people who wish to self-publish or co-publish their works.

Gerard continues to offer lectures on "You Are Your Spiritual Workplace," "Living the Moment: Experiencing Freedom," and "Spirituality in the Workplace" as his focus. He may be contacted with regard to his lectures and workshops at:

OUGHTEN HOUSE FOUNDATION, INC.
P.O. Box 3134
LIVERMORE, CALIFORNIA 94551-3134 USA
(510) 447-2372
FAX (510) 447-2376
E-MAIL: oughtenhouse.com
INTERNET: www.oughtenhouse.com

Books for the Rising Planetary Consciousness

The Crystal Stair: A Guide to the Ascension, by Eric Klein. A collection of channeled teachings received from Lord Sananda (Jesus) and other Masters, describing the personal and planetary ascension process now actively occurring on our planet.

— *ISBN 1-880666-06-5, $12.95*

The Inner Door: Channeled Discourses from the Ascended Masters on Self-Mastery and Ascension, by Eric Klein. In these two volumes, intended as a sequel to *The Crystal Stair,* the Masters address the challenges of the journey to ascension.

— *Volume One: ISBN 1-880666-03-0, $14.50*
— *Volume Two: ISBN 1-880666-16-2, $14.50*

Jewels on the Path: Transformational Teachings of the Ascended Masters, by Eric Klein. In this book, the ideas and themes introduced in Klein's earlier books are clarified and refined to bring you up to date on the ascension process and how to be a more active participant. This is the best one yet!

— *ISBN 1-880666-48-0, $13.50*

An Ascension Handbook, by Tony Stubbs. A practical presentation which describes the ascension process in detail and includes several exercises to help you integrate it into your daily life.

— *ISBN 1-880666-08-1, $12.95*

Bridge Into Light: Your Connection to Spiritual Guidance, by Pam and Fred Cameron. Lovingly offers many step-by-step exercises on how to meditate and how to channel, and gives ways to invoke the protection and assistance of the Masters. Companion tape available.

— *ISBN 1-880666-07-3, $11.95*

What Is Lightbody? by Tashira Tachi-ren offers a twelve-level model for the ascension process, leading to the attainment of our Lightbody. Recommended in *An Ascension Handbook*, this book gives many invocations, procedures, and potions to assist us on our journey home. (Related tapes available.)

— *ISBN 1-880666-25-1, $12.95*

Lady From Atlantis, by Robert V. Gerard. Shar Dae, the future Empress of Atlantis, is suddenly transported onto a rain-soaked beach in modern America. There she meets her twin flame and discovers her mission: to warn the people of planet Earth to mend their ways before Mother Earth takes matters in her own hands!

— *ISBN 1-880666-21-9, $12.95*

Intuition by Design, by Victor R. Beasley, Ph.D. A boxed set of 36 IQ (Intuition Quotient) Cards contain consciousness-changing geometry on one side and transformational verse on the other. The companion book tells you the many ways to use the cards in all aspects of your life. An incredible gift to yourself and someone you love. Bring your life into alignment with the Higher Mind of Source.

— *ISBN 1-880666-22-7, $21.95*

The Extraterrestrial Vision by Gina Lake. Through Gina, Theodore, a nonphysical entity, tells us what we need to know about our extraterrestrial heritage and how to prepare for direct contact with those civilizations which will soon be appearing in our midst.

— *ISBN 1-880666-19-7, $13.95*

ET Contact: Blueprint for a New World, by Gina Lake. Through Gina, the Confederation of Planets tells us what life on Earth will be like following mass contact with extraterrestrials, and what we must do to prepare for life with ETs.

— *ISBN 1-880666-62-6, $12.95*

Navigating the 90s by Deborah Soucek. Practical ways to deal with today's chaotic times, and claim your sovereignty when others would trample it. Packed with pertinent observations and useful exercises.
— *ISBN 1-880666-47-2, $13.95*

Angels of the Rays by Johanna. A set of twelve lavish, full color Angel pictures with supporting descriptions and invocations. Includes a push-out color card for each Angel. *Makes a stunning gift!*
— *ISBN 1-880666-34-0, $19.95. (Additional card sets $12.95)*

Voice in the Mirror: Will The Final Apocalypse Be Averted? by Lee Shargel. In this first novel of *The Chulosian Chronicles*, Lee skilfully weaves fact and fiction to tell a thrilling story of extra-terrestrials using the Hubble telescope to warn of impending planetary disaster. But that's only the beginning!
— *ISBN 1-880666-54-5, $23.95 (hardcover).*

Attention: Businesses and Schools!

OUGHTEN HOUSE books are available at quantity discounts with bulk purchases for educational, business, or sales promotional use. For details, please contact the publisher.

CATALOG REQUESTS & BOOK ORDERS

Catalogs will gladly be sent upon request. Book orders must be prepaid: check, money order, international coupon, VISA,
To place your order, call, fax, or mail to:

OUGHTEN HOUSE PUBLICATIONS
PO Box 2008
LIVERMORE · CALIFORNIA · 94551-2008 · USA
PHONE: (510) 447-2332
Fax: (510) 447-2376
E-MAIL: oughtenhouse.com
INTERNET: www.oughtenhouse.com

Handling Verbal Confrontation
Take the Fear Out of Facing Others
by Robert V. Gerard

A hard-hitting, no-punches-pulled, workshop-style book that presents a new way of dramatically improving interpersonal confrontation skills and explains why current ways don't work.

Handling Verbal Confrontation, with the aid of clear diagrams and proven techniques, gives step-by-step guidance on how to strategically prepare for a verbal confrontation, conduct a confrontation session, and produce a win-win-win outcome that benefits your company or your marriage. And the techniques are an investment that will pay off for the rest of your life!

Whether the confrontation occurs at home or work, these sure-fire methods guarantee that both parties will be heard, and that accountability for problem-solving and further action will be properly assigned.

Handling Verbal Confrontation will change the way you conduct just about every interaction with people, and most important, with yourself. One of the main reasons why confrontations end up as shouting matches that solve nothing is because you haven't first confronted yourself on the issue at hand. So before you confront anyone else, you must first be clear on where you stand, and then strategically confront to achieve the required change. *Handling Verbal Confrontation* tells you how!

Handling Verbal Confrontation is backed by lectures and workshops conducted by the author and his staff of qualified trainers at your site or ours.

To order the book (available summer 1997), or arrange a seminar or workshop call Oughten House.

— *ISBN 1-880666-05-7 $14.95 (7 x 10 trade paperback)*